Healing *from* Family Rifts

Ten Steps to Finding Peace After Being Cut Off from a Family Member

Mark Sichel, CSW

McGraw·Hill

New York   Chicago   San Francisco   Lisbon   London   Madrid   Mexico City
Milan   New Delhi   San Juan   Seoul   Singapore   Sydney   Toronto

Library of Congress Cataloging-in-Publication Data

Sichel, Mark.
      Healing from family rifts : ten steps to finding peace after being cut off from a family
member / Mark Sichel.—1st ed.
         p.   cm.
      Includes index.
      ISBN 0-07-141242-5 (alk. paper)
      1. Family.   2. Interpersonal relations.   I. Title.

HQ519.S53   2004
305.85—dc22   2003018017

1 2 3 4 5 6 7 8 9 0   DOC/DOC   3 2 1 0 9 8 7 6 5 4

ISBN 0-07-141242-5

McGraw-Hill books are available at special quantity discounts to use as premiums and sales
promotions, or for use in corporate training programs. For more information, please write to
the Director of Special Sales, Professional Publishing, McGraw-Hill, Two Penn Plaza,
New York, NY 10121-2298. Or contact your local bookstore.

This book is printed on acid-free paper.

Contents

Acknowledgments

I am deeply grateful to my wife and best friend, Cindy Kasovitz Sichel, who never ceases to amaze and inspire me. Her encouragement, support, and generosity have made this book possible. I am thankful to her as well for serving as a model to our children, Steven and Kenneth Sichel, Jeanne and Ross Kasovitz; they are all truly a gift that never stops giving.

My deepest appreciation goes also to Guy Blake Kettelhack, my editorial collaborator and wise writing mentor; Stephanie Von Hirschberg, my literary agent who had the courage and wisdom to support this project; and to Judith McCarthy, my editor at McGraw-Hill whose clarity and vision provided me with the structure to complete this work.

I owe a deep debt to the many clients who entrusted me to collaborate in their efforts to make sense out of their experiences, and whose struggles and triumphs continue to deepen my understanding of life, love, and family.

Last, I want to thank the members of my second-chance family, whose influence and support have been life sustaining, especially Tess Rosenfeld, Lisa and Lloyd Zeiderman, Cheryl, Randall, and Amanda Rothenberg, and my friend and brother Thomas Glasser and all the other heroes who gave their lives on September 11, 2001, so that we may continue to live in freedom and dignity.

Introduction

Stopping the War

"That's it. I've had it. I never want to see or hear from you again."

These words are terrible, whoever says them. But when they come from your mother, father, son, daughter, sister, brother, or spouse—or when you find yourself saying them yourself to a family member—you know, for the moment, what hell is like.

Maybe not right off. Maybe you even feel relief, a rush of justifiable anger armoring you against the assault you've just received or given. Angry banishments don't come from nowhere. They usually erupt out of years of backed-up resentments, long-held grudges. They may follow intolerable mental, emotional or physical abuse. In fact, at least in the short term, sometimes they can mark a much-needed release and relief ("Thank God I don't have to deal with him anymore . . .").

But soon, however justified or inevitable the explosion may have seemed, however determinedly resigned you may have tried to be about a family cut-off, feelings almost always start to change. Bad dreams may haunt you. Toxic resentments and regrets increase with a sickening resurgence ("How could he?" "How could she?" or "How could I have said that to her [or to him]?"); now they really won't let you go. Guilt flips to vengeful fantasy, self-righteous indignation to shame, rage to depression and back again. However shaky your family's bonds may have been to begin with, however little or much love you may have felt toward or from them over the years, the idea that those bonds have been eradicated almost always wreaks a terrible havoc.

When we deal with family, we deal with some of our most deeply entrenched fears and yearnings. The parent/child relationship in particular is mightily charged. Losing a mother or father or child or sibling as the result of family exile can be as traumatic as losing them to death. Sometimes a good deal more, because death, at least, is usually not seen as anyone's "fault." Whatever we may say that we feel or think or believe about our families, almost inevitably—deep down—we yearn for connection to them.

If you've picked up this book, it's likely you know this already. You've already had a taste of the despair of feeling severed from ties that once—perhaps very long ago, perhaps not so long ago—you probably never believed could break as irreparably as they may appear to have broken now.

Maybe the worst part is the secrecy—the feeling that you couldn't possibly tell anyone what you're going through. A family is supposed to mean love, not hate. How could you admit to anyone what you've seen and heard your family do and say? *Dysfunctional* doesn't begin to say it. Almost every family rift causes deep shame and embarrassment.

So—typically—you don't talk about it. You may barely allow yourself to think about it. Maybe you try to ignore it, tell yourself to "snap out of it" or otherwise white-knuckle yourself into pretending that all will be well if you can just hang on long enough—put your mind on something else. But even if you manage to put up a good show, inside it's not working. I don't have to tell you this. You wouldn't have picked up this book if it were otherwise.

There Is a Way Out

Let me assure you now that things can get better. The isolation of family exile has an exit. And this book will enable you to find it.

Your family circumstances do not matter—who has caused the rift, whom you perceive to be the victim or victimizer, what your role in the break has been, what you see as the reasons for the cutoff (money, religion, drugs, alcohol, sex, sexual orientation, race, social status, age, abuse, mental illness, divorce, remarriage, stepfamilies, or any other circumstance). If you give yourself over to the steps in this book, you can—and will—heal from it.

How can I be so sure there is a way out? First, because I've experienced it in my own life. Second, I see the process work daily in the lives of patients and friends who've come to me thinking there was no way any "process" could work—no way they could possibly recover from the devastation of feeling permanently booted out of the family nest. And yet they do all discover an eventual healing.

I am a therapist who has worked with many people in this situation, and I have experienced a family rift myself. I am not a guru. The lessons that this book will pass on to you weren't bestowed upon me in a great epiphany from on high. Not that they don't have what I call "spiritual" components—they do. But basically they arise out of the hard work and often unforeseen joys of daily life—and of having to deal personally with the problems this book addresses. I'm a family and individual therapist, a father and husband, and the son of parents who have, since January 2001, severed all contact with me. The experience of dealing with my own pain of family exile—the deep self-reflection it has engendered and the jolts of seeing the paths my similarly cut-off patients have taken—all ultimately have helped me to forge and codify ten steps to reconciling from family rifts. I'll share those ten steps with you here.

You'll hear my own story along with those of a rich and amazingly varied range of other embattled survivors of family wars, as they went through each step of healing the book offers and worked through what we each once felt to be intractable, untenable, unworkable family messes. You'll see how we've begun to achieve real inner reconciliation. You'll see that whether you're able to reconcile with your family of origin, or find that for now you must maintain distance from them, you can achieve serenity and contentment because you'll have learned to free yourself from toxic and dysfunctional patterns. You'll learn the principles we've drawn from our own often disparate circumstances and difficulties—principles that deliver up daily, moment by moment, the path to healing. Then you'll learn how to make it work in your own life.

You'll also learn that the most important "reconciliation" is the one you learn to make with yourself. All healing proceeds from that.

Here is the bare-bones plan of what this healing entails:

The Ten Steps of—and Stops on the Ride to—Reconciling Family Rifts
1. Acknowledge and deal with the shock.
2. Start to live, laugh, and be happy *now*.
3. Discover your family roles.
4. Understand your family myths.
5. Learn from successful families.
6. Let go of resentment.

7. Make the first move: learn and employ active measures to reconcile with your family.
8. Build your second-chance family.
9. Cultivate gratitude and emotional generosity.
10. Make meaning out of your experience.

The language in some of these steps will no doubt seem familiar to you. How many times, for example, have you heard "let go of resentments" or "make the first move" (take the initiative) or "find peace within yourself"? But as you'll see in a moment, this book's take on these steps has its surprises.

Part of the heart of what makes this approach work is that it doesn't involve slogging through a lot of heavy analysis or navel-gazing—nor is the "good stuff" kept until last. This program is not a matter of forcing you to eat your liver and lima beans before you get to the ice cream sundae at the end. Look at Step Two: "Start to live, laugh, and be happy *now*." Let's strike that very positive note right off: that you can take measures, probably sooner than you think, to turn your attitudes around right now—not only your attitudes about family, but, maybe more importantly, your attitudes about yourself and your own prospects for happiness.

Join me in finding out how.

1

Acknowledge and Deal
with the Shock

Whether you've been cut off by your family, or you've cut off a family member because of circumstances you find intolerable, you invariably undergo a traumatic shock. Certainly my father's wholesale rejection of me shook me to my core—a trauma I've since learned had a number of stages I had first to acknowledge, and then to navigate. How I've managed to weather and overcome the worst of this trauma—and how my patients have similarly learned to prevail over what is often an initial indescribable agony of a family rift—offer the substance of this first chapter, which describes the first step in healing.

A good deal of the shock for me came from the unnerving realization that my usual reliable approach to dealing with crisis—thinking my way through it, and reaching a sense of how to cope with it—just wasn't working here. I developed symptoms of dysfunction that were uncharacteristic of me—I felt unanchored, cheated, disgusted, full of shame, self-doubt, sadness, guilt, and fear—toxic emotions that engendered a terrible sense of confusion and powerlessness. Soon I was able to see that most of these symptoms signaled acute stress disorder, a diagnosis that ultimately suggested ways I could begin to heal.

Fortunately, one certainty born of my clinical experience and the lessons of having dealt with other difficult situations in my life hadn't deserted me. I knew that the initial level of toxic intensity and functional impairment I felt would eventually pass. It always does when you do the right things for yourself.

Understanding the Trauma Is of Human Design

The first "right thing" was simply this: I needed to remind myself not to trivialize or attempt to minimize the effects of what I was going through—I had instead to give it its full due. Family estrangement on some level seemed "logically" to be less catastrophic than some of the terrible things going on in the world such as terrorist attacks, violent crime, natural disasters such as fire or earthquakes, or the actual physical death of a loved one. However, it had a magnitude *for me* that, at least for the moment, far exceeded these catastrophes. I needed to accept this—and to be careful not to add to an already festering sense of shame and guilt (flip sides of my rage and hurt) that I was somehow "over-reacting"—that "it could be worse." Hypothetically, of course, there's always something that "could be worse," but the impact of my father severing contact with me had, especially in the fresh wake of the cutoff, subjected me to the worst emotional trauma I could remember ever undergoing. I couldn't underestimate the impact of this trauma—or chastise myself for overreacting. This wasn't the time to judge my feelings—to attempt artificially to gloss over the pain. This wasn't the time to blame myself for the sudden incapacities the trauma caused in my life. This was the time to let myself feel it, all of it—and acknowledge it.

Part of acknowledging it meant understanding that the trauma *was* so great because it had been caused by human beings—it hadn't come from chance, or an act of God—it had come through *human* choice. All traumas are more magnified and psychologically upsetting when human beings rather than nature cause them. Losing your home to a fire will certainly be traumatic, but losing it because arsonists caused the fire will almost always make the effects of the shock more severe. Similarly, the trauma of a family member physically dying usually becomes less painful with time—it falls under the heading of a natural catastrophe from which the human psyche ultimately learns to heal. However, on two decades of evidence of the scores of my patients who've faced both kinds of trauma, the psychological "death" of a family cutoff clearly tends to remain torturous—and very much more emotionally damaging. Obviously family cutoffs are not the only devastating traumas we commonly face. Divorce, for example, can be every bit as disruptive. But unlike most family cutoffs, divorce has at least some social acceptance: it is talked about much more readily than other cutoffs in the family tend to be.

This suggests what compounds the problem: the terrible secrecy that usually attends family cutoffs—and the related fact that there is very little formal help offered to people who've undergone them. Many family members feel self-imposed pressure to go on as if their lives were still normal; thus, avenues for healing and recovery become even more elusive. After all, this trauma isn't only of human design—it's the design of *members of your own family*: the very people you thought loved you most in the world. That isn't something you're likely to broadcast—or even tell most of your best friends in private.

However, you *need* to talk right now, and to recognize that the task of healing from your family rift will take a much greater effort than you probably have ever previously brought to emotional distress in your life. With the right attitude of self-compassion, and by employing tactics you will learn in this book, it is fortunately an effort immeasurably worth taking.

You Don't Have to Fix or Resolve Anything Today

It's normal to want closure after something as terrible as a family rift—indeed, our impulse may be to do anything possible to make the pain go away, whether it involves abject and inappropriate apologies (amounting to groveling to keep the peace) or resorting to drugs or alcohol to help you escape the pain. However, a necessary corollary to understanding that you're dealing with trauma of a completely different order than you have probably faced before is understanding that this healing is going to take time. There are no quick fixes here: there couldn't be, given our natural human aversion to ambiguity and uncertainty coupled with what are generally the lifelong roots of dysfunction that led to your family rift in the first place. In short, now's the time to give yourself permission to *go slow*. You don't have to fix or resolve anything today.

This means having compassion for yourself—and especially for the impetus that makes you crave quick closure: the inability to tolerate mixed feelings of love, hate, longing, rage, sadness, and vengeance. A family cutoff is initially a phenomenally confusing time for all concerned; this degree of uncertainty is not easy for anyone. However, I can tell you from years of practicing psychotherapy that, as uncomfortable as it is, confusion is actually necessary for growth. It's out of the flux of life that we're often able to question old self-limiting assumptions and begin the journey to changing our attitudes and behavior—to begin, in other words, to heal, even from something as devastating as a family rift.

When It Feels like You've Been Buried Alive

"Buried alive" isn't invariably the phrase used by people who undergo the trauma of a family cutoff—sometimes it's more along the lines of "It's like some major part of me has gone dead," or "I feel shattered by this—like I don't know what's *real* anymore." But "buried alive" is a good way of summing up the feeling of dissociation you often feel after the family rift. Being cut off from the family so often devolves into feeling cut off from something central in yourself.

Lori offers a typical example. She came into therapy initially to get over the effects of a devastating divorce. Married for ten years, Lori finally summoned up the courage to walk away from her husband when his abuse—which had crossed the line from verbal to physical—became dangerous to her and their six-year-old son Ryan. Over some months, she had managed to build her strength and confidence back to the point where she could begin to understand why she had put up with her violent husband's treatment. As with many battered spouses, she had put up with similar treatment as a child from her father, and realized she was caught in a repetition of seeking out a man whose unpredictably fiery temperament mirrored her father's. "It's the old story," she said. "It was the only kind of attention from a man I knew, so I obviously sought it out again." She had also begun to develop patience with herself about how long it would take to change course and heal more completely from the effects of violence in her family life.

She sent her son to a child psychiatrist for treatment as well—a therapist recommended to her by her younger sister Arlene, to whom she felt indebted for this show of concern and support, especially since growing up they had never been close. "Arlene had been the favorite—my father never punished her the way he punished me. And yet somehow she'd always been jealous of me—especially because she wanted to get married and have kids, and it just hadn't worked out for her. I always felt after Ryan was born that this envy just increased—she wanted a 'Ryan' too. So her helping me right now with getting Ryan help after the divorce gave me hope that maybe she'd gotten over her feelings of resentment."

Then came a new, and in many ways far more terrible, shock. Her sister and mother kidnapped Ryan and brought him to live with her ex-husband after learning that Ryan's psychiatrist had reported her to the Bureau of Children's Protective Services, charging that Lori was clinically depressed, abusing drugs, and unable to be a fit mother.

"I thought going through a divorce was hard, but now I've really been brought to my knees by what my sister and mother did to me. It turned out the support I thought I was getting from Arlene was anything but. It was a setup—she was determined to get my son away from me, as some crazy act of vengeance. I just can't understand the charges—what could they have been thinking? They knew I had gone on an antidepressant as part of therapy, but I was hardly a drug addict. All I can think is that whatever distress signals Ryan was sending out to the psychiatrist must somehow have been embellished and twisted by Arlene, who also even convinced my mother that I was 'unfit.'"

Almost as bad as losing Ryan was the feeling that her family literally wanted Lori dead. "They couldn't have hurt me more if they'd just aimed a gun at my heart and pulled the trigger. It's like whatever world of family safety I thought I was in shattered." Lori reported a dream she'd had shortly after this debacle that patently arose from these feelings of being gunned down. "I dreamed that I was being shot, executioner style. I was on my knees, facing away from the executioner. I heard the gun explode—but instead of bullets shooting into me, I was hit by a siege of beads, the kind used for costume jewelry." Lori's mother owned a bead, sequin, and fashion accessory company in the garment district of New York. "The beads stung me," Lori said, "but they didn't kill me. I remember in the dream feeling terribly upset—but knowing somehow I would be okay. I woke up, however, terror-struck. I got no sleep for the rest of the night. I'm still exhausted, scared, confused, angry. Even though I know my mother's 'beads' won't kill me, the fact that she and Arlene have gone through the motions of executing me is just intolerable. In a way, I feel like *I* was shot out of a gun, and landed somewhere, alone, terribly remote from anything I thought I knew."

Acute Stress Disorder

Lori's story, while different in specifics, resonates strongly with other victims of family rifts I've worked with, and with my own experience. I too felt that my family war would kill me, and it took some work to know I'd survive and be fine. Here's the flag of reassurance—one that Lori's dream had also explicitly offered her (she was shot by beads, not bullets: hurt but not killed): You are not having a life-threatening emergency, as you might feel. You are more than likely suffering from acute stress disorder. I had it, Lori had it, and you probably have or have had it.

Remember that, like the people you will read about in this book, you too will survive and, at the end of working on these steps, find ways to heal from whatever blows the family rift has caused you. The stakes often feel like life or death, but they aren't. If you know you're doing everything in your power to mend the situation, it can't kill you. In fact, grappling with the trauma can breathe new hope and strength into your life in many unsuspected ways.

"At Least I'm Not Going Crazy . . ."

Jason's experience is an interesting case-in-point: learning not only that we can survive the terrible toxicity of a family cutoff, but that in the very seeds of what we often feel has nearly destroyed our hearts and senses of self are clues about the real situation we face (as opposed to the killing nightmare it may at first seem to us)—clues even about how to heal from it.

However, as Jason would be the first to tell you, this ability to feel hope in the midst of despair can be a long time coming. The oldest of three sons, Jason had always been the light of his parents' life—an accomplished athlete, magna cum laude graduate of an Ivy League school, and now a successful copywriter at a major advertising agency. His two younger brothers had floundered by comparison: one struggled with intermittent drug problems, the other with chronic depression. "I knew my poor brothers constantly felt compared to me—a sort of 'why can't you be more like Jason?' thing that my parents constantly subjected them to. It made me feel really uncomfortable. Especially since I wasn't quite the person my parents believed I was."

Unbeknownst to his parents, Jason is gay. And now, in his late thirties, he was tired of hiding it. "I'd felt so much family pressure to be the Perfect Child that I didn't dare let my parents know about my sexuality. I guess I didn't realize how much I had invested in keeping up appearances with them. They're both super-conservative and I knew how they would likely feel about finding out one of their sons was gay. But it was finally taking way too much of a toll on me. So when I met my partner Oliver, and the relationship deepened to the point that we knew we wanted to get as close to married as society would allow us, I finally made the decision to 'fess up to my family."

Jason says he realizes his way of doing this probably wasn't the wisest course he could have taken, but as he also says, "It felt like diving into a pool. You either dive or you don't. I guess I wanted to be absolutely clear—and give them the news without mincing words. So, without warning, I sent my parents an invitation to the commitment ceremony Oliver and I planned—in other words, I invited them to their firstborn son's gay wedding."

Jason will always remember the phone call he received in response. "My father's voice was trembling with rage and hurt. 'As far as your mother and I are concerned,' he said in the scariest voice I'd ever heard him use, 'we do not have three sons. We have two. Unless you get help to become a normal man, we will have nothing to do with you.'" Jason visibly pales as he recounts this. "Then my mother got on the line. I couldn't believe the abuse she hurled at me—in a way it was much worse even than my father's abrupt dismissal. Homosexuality was reprehensible, a sin against God—the whole conservative Bible Belt nine yards. She said I was doomed to hell unless I sought help."

Jason was a mess for weeks after this. "Thank God I had Oliver and a family of close friends to help get me through that time. Oliver especially was amazing. It was he who really pushed me to seek therapy—he could feel how damaged I felt inside, and he knew it was an emotional emergency. Sort of like I needed triage that he knew even his great love for me wasn't equipped to provide. He said, 'It's like they cut off one of your arms. All I could think of was, you needed to go to a psychological ER. I couldn't stand to watch you bleed like that.'" Hence, Oliver's suggestion that Jason come to me. But Jason did not come to me primarily for help with rage and hurt. It was his sudden inability to feel anything at all.

"I feel like I'm dead," Jason said. "I wish I could cry or scream or something. But actually right now I don't know what I feel. It's like I'm wrapped up like a mummy against my feelings—like there's some huge open wound that goes so deep and is so far gone with nerve damage that the patient doesn't feel any pain. I've tried to break through this numbness with my old resolve to 'act.' After I couldn't sleep last night, I decided—ridiculously—to get up early this morning and go running, thinking that it would clear my head.

"I could see, distantly, it was a beautiful morning, but I couldn't feel it. As I ran—exhausted, sleepless—all I could do was replay that phone call in my head, going over every word of it, wondering what I might have said differently, scouring their invective for some clue about what had happened and why they had withdrawn their love for me so violently. I thought these things rather than felt them. Like some terrible compulsion, I went over and over and over it, and got nowhere. I swung wildly from thinking they were monsters to thinking I was a monster. Then I tried to make contact with my feelings for Oliver—but even that seemed so remote now. In the middle of the compulsive buzz in my head, I just couldn't feel anything."

Symptoms of Acute Stress Disorder

The rat-in-a-cage emotional rut that Jason describes is a strikingly common reaction to the violence of a family cutoff, as is Jason's inability to feel the rage and hurt and terror he distantly knows is somewhere in him. "This buzz of words in my head, but no real feeling attached to them—it's like hell," he said. Exhausted from his run and sleepless night, Jason then pushed himself through a day at work. "The buzz just wouldn't let up. I tried to make how my parents had treated me square with who I thought—I guess hoped—they really were. That disjunction permeates everything in my life now—it's like I've lost trust in anyone who says they love me. Even sometimes Oliver . . . It's like there's suddenly this whole new awful negative identity that has blocked everything in me I used to be so proud and happy about. When I tried to concentrate on work, it was all a blur. It's as if I had been hacked to pieces, which had been scattered all around me, and I couldn't imagine how to bring them all back, how to be whole again."

The clinical term for the symptoms Jason reports, as I've already suggested, is *acute distress disorder*. As with other people I have either treated or interviewed who've gone through the family exile experience, it is unfortunately very common. It's always accompanied by at least several of the following:

- Numbness
- Detachment

- Unresponsiveness
- Depersonalization
- Dissociativeness
- Compulsive rumination
- Repeatedly reexperiencing the "final conversation"
- Dreams of the shattering event
- Sleep or eating difficulties
- Avoidance of people, places, or things that bring back the memory of the trauma
- Impairment of social and occupational functioning
- Inability to concentrate, lack of focus
- Restlessness, irritability
- Anhedonia (inability to experience pleasure)

Jason had experienced every one of these symptoms, and, seeing the list of them, said he felt strangely reassured: "So how I'm feeling is normal?" He let out the first almost peaceful sigh I'd heard from him: "At least I'm not going crazy." I could reassure him further: based on my experience and that of all the people I'd worked with who similarly suffered from the disorder, the worst of these symptoms would very likely disappear in fairly short order. They were protective defenses: tactics his psyche had resorted to reflexively to buffer him against the fresh trauma. This suggested that he might not only want to accept that he was feeling "numb" now, when he was—but be grateful for it. And he should understand that his general reactions at this moment by no means comprised the last "act" in the family rift play into which he'd suddenly been plunged.

Part of this reassurance contained a gentle warning, however: while most of the debilitating symptoms of acute stress disorder can be counted on to fade in relatively short order, the underlying trauma will of course take much longer to deal with. Aspects of it probably will resurface at various future times. The good news is that we have—and we *will* have—more resources to deal with it than we realize in the immediate aftermath of the break.

In fact, when effects or memories of a trauma resurface, it's often the psyche's signal that the underlying wound they arise from needs to be dealt with in new ways. If we don't tend to it, that wound can continue to toxify our reactions to life over many years to come. I recently received a query on my website Psybersquare.com from a woman who had suddenly begun to reexperience symptoms from a family break that had happened thirty years before. Her mother and ex-husband had her committed to a mental hospital in 1973, and she was confined there for three days with the task of proving her sanity to the staff. She evidently managed to do this, since they released her at the end of her allotted lockup. After this, she had managed to go on and create a new family and career for herself. She'd gotten remarried, had children and grandchildren, and had just retired from her job when she contacted me. Now, all of a sudden, she said, she found herself obsessively reliving her mother's betrayal and rejection of her, and she couldn't stop ruminating over the details.

In every stage of life we are challenged by new psychological tasks, and often, as we face and prepare for a major life event—like this woman's retirement—whatever unresolved business we may have in our past lives rears up with particular and sometimes very disturbing force. This woman had, in her life, responded to her family's abrupt estrangement quite effectively after it happened, but she had never sufficiently dealt with it emotionally. The good news, I was able to report to her now, is that her psyche had allowed the pain to resurface at a time when she was strong and wise enough to be able to tolerate, understand and deal with it.

This suggests an interesting point about trauma worth recalling: we can expect some of its effects—especially those we have not faced adequately (and none of us faces all of them perfectly)—to resurface at certain (often big-event) moments of life, even many years after the fact. Whether pleasant or unpleasant (the birth of a child or grandchild, a wedding, or a national tragedy like that of September 11, 2001), landmark events typically kick up traumatic recall. The best watchword here is patience—respecting that our psyches, like those of Jason and this just-retired woman, not only often ingeniously protect themselves from too much pain at the time the trauma is inflicted, but wait for us to encounter more buried effects of that pain later, when we are strong enough to deal with it. However, when it comes up again, we really *must* deal with it—or its latent toxicity will continue to eat away at our lives.

Why We Often "Go Crazy" After a Family Rift

To some degree, just from what we've seen so far, you already know the answer to this implicit question. When we feel we've "lost it" or "gone crazy" or "can't feel anything," we're experiencing very normal symptoms of trauma. Numbness is especially common—its self-protective function is to distract us from the worst excesses of our pain. But there's more to why we experience the specific symptoms each of us evinces after a family cutoff—symptoms (as in the above list) that can range widely. You'll be helped to acknowledge and deal with the trauma you're undergoing by understanding a bit more about how and why that trauma is affecting you in the particular ways it is.

What is known as the *ego* in psychoanalytic theory describes the area of the personality that powers our psyche—the part that tells us what to do and when to do it, the chief executive officer who operates and competes in the outer world. The strength of our ego is based on the sum power of our psychological muscle. Ego represents a group of functions that as a whole reflect overall psychological strength—the ability to exert our wills to get what we want.

Actually there are many ego functions that we use all the time, but the specific ones that become impaired in response to a traumatic crisis are mastery and competence, ability to delay gratification, and tolerance for frustration. Just as a physical assault creates bodily damage, a psychological attack can damage our ability to use our ego strength to full capacity. In the aftermath of a family estrangement, we do not generally feel masterful or competent, which leads to an unsettling feeling of loss of control. We want solutions, and we want them now. The frustration of not being able to come to quick solutions is part of what fuels the obsessive ruminations that we've already seen as symptoms suffered by Jason and my Psybersquare woman—a feeling of being trapped in impotence that can become unbearable.

Another major ego function commonly crippled by the assault of a family rift is the ability to process strong emotions. When we're shocked, it takes us time to learn how to manage our feelings. When we can't tolerate the strength of them, we become vulnerable not only to obsessive ruminations and thoughts, but also to intermittent stages of emotional turnoff—where (as when Jason reported the "buzz" of words in his head as well as his numbness) we don't feel anything at all. It's as if the psyche continually, repetitively goes over the same route of attack and retreat—again and again, despite the fact that such a swing offers no lasting solution or relief. Obsessive rumination, however, is particularly toxic. And while it's important to acknowledge, as Jason did, that it's a completely normal symptom in the context of a family cutoff—what, apart from tolerating it, can you do about it?

What to Do About the Symptoms of Acute Stress Disorder

First, remember that you're still at a stage of needing psychological first-aid. Think of yourself as in a hospital emergency room—the first task is to stop the bleeding and contain the wound. This means, of course, first acknowledging that you *have* a wound. But it quickly requires something else. You are already familiar with some of these resources. Recall the activities that you know from past experience will soothe you. This is the time to make the popcorn, draw the bubble bath, watch the movie, get the massage, play the game of tennis, read the novel that you know can offer at least a bit of respite. Call them psychological band-aids if you want, but if they work, use them now— as long as they don't make the situation worse, which generally means, as long as they're not self-destructive (such as alcohol, drugs, or overeating).

Soothe yourself as you can. Think of it as spreading the blanket on the bed and fluffing up the pillow. This is preparation for the real work of acknowledgment, which is simply this: to talk until you're blue in the face. A lot has built up inside you—and it all (or as much of it as you can tolerate) must come out.

Productive Talk: Choose Your "Ear" Wisely

Asked about what helps a person get over trauma, the vast majority of mental health professionals will agree that talking about it is by far the treatment of choice. But how can the talk be made productive—so that it's not just a compulsive rehashing of "how could they?" or "why didn't I?"

Some of what you need to let out will be, in fact, the "how could they?" or "why didn't I?" brands of reaction you'll inevitably have. The point here isn't to censor you—it's to beckon you to release everything about your trauma that you've felt you must hold back. There are, as you'll see in a moment, ways to encourage yourself to get beyond that blame-or-defense mode, but right now, it's more important to focus on something else: whom you choose to let it all out to.

Some listeners are better for this task than others. It's tempting to find someone who will side with you—echo and confirm every last thing you say. Indeed the comforts of having someone around who seems to agree totally with your side of the story are undeniable: for the moment, at least, they can make you feel vindicated. However, a yes-man or yes-woman isn't as helpful as someone who is equally caring but more dispassionate, even if all you want and need right now is someone to vent to. (Suggestions about how to find this caring, dispassionate someone are coming up.)

Equally important is to find someone who isn't trigger-happy with advice. Right now, some very basic advice may be welcome and helpful (listen, for example, to friends who know you haven't been sleeping or eating and who want to help you take care of your physical well-being). However, most advice—particularly from people who vent their own distress by giving advice (usually as a tactic to dismiss or get rid of you)—isn't what's called for now. What's called for is someone, or a group of people, you can depend on to listen to you without barging in unduly or subjecting you to unwanted opinions, judgments, or expectations. No human being is a perfect listener, but some are better than others, and right now you need the best you can get.

Let's first do a quick survey of different categories of listeners—some of which may turn out to be more helpful than they may appear to be at first glance.

Friends and Family: Sometimes Support Is in Your Own Backyard

Linda came into therapy to talk about how to deal with her daughter Anne's estrangement from the family because of her involvement—"brainwashing," Linda said—in a therapeutic cult. Linda found she not only needed to vent, but she needed to make contact, and talk about her secret fears and guilts, with her husband Ted and her other daughter Liz. One suggestion I made to her was for the three of them to go to a support group for families who had lost children to cults.

"Once we got into the support group and found other parents who had also lost their kids in the way we felt we'd lost Anne, we not only felt less alone—we became accustomed to talking about it more openly. This had always been a secret we'd kept from nearly everyone we knew—having a place to air even our worst worries and fears and confusions has been unbelievably healing. And not only in the context of the support group. As we felt less shameful about what had happened, we could start talking to other relatives and friends—and were overcome by how loving and supportive they were.

There simply was more help to be had than we knew. Not the least of this is that Ted, Liz, and I are closer for having shared our pain and anger and distress."

You can find similar support for yourself in so many places. A considerable perk of finding it in support groups with other members of your family is that you learn tools others have used to get through the worst of what you too are facing. But even if there's no self-help group appropriate to the family rift drama you're undergoing, don't forget that members of your family with whom you're still close, and friends you've confided in about other difficulties you've faced, will often be able to provide wonderful ears right now, when you need someone to listen to most of all.

Clergy: Spiritual Listening and Guidance

I spent many years teaching clergy how to do family counseling, and I'm always surprised at how few people of every faith avail themselves of this resource. This holds true particularly in a family estrangement crisis, because being cut off by a family member shakes your spiritual foundation as much as your mental or psychological one. When my parents refused to attend my youngest son's bar mitzvah, my wife and I went to speak with our rabbi on a number of occasions. Although we never formalized the contact as "psychotherapy," it certainly proved therapeutic to both of us.

Many people resist the idea of turning to clergy because they're afraid they'll get dogma and banal palliatives. However, many clergy offer so much more wisdom than you may expect: these days they're trained to listen, and the best of them can offer a comfort far more profound than you may be able to find anywhere else.

Shirley, an eighty-year old woman and mother of six children who had all grown up and married and led their lives elsewhere for many years, was devastated a few years ago when her daughter Kate cut off all contact with her. The only explanation Shirley received was that it was "for reasons that ought to be obvious." "I just can't imagine what those reasons are," Shirley said. "It's true I divorced her father—who ran out on me in my fifties for a younger woman—and I remarried afterwards. But Kate always knew the circumstances of the divorce, and I thought had always sided with me. Anyway, that was thirty years ago. There was no obvious enmity between Kate and my second husband—who died four years ago—before Kate decided to drop the guillotine. I just don't have a clue what happened. She won't answer any of my calls or letters. . . ."

Shirley was in such despair over this that she had lost all pleasure in life. "This was such a blow to me that I almost stopped wanting to live. It was then that I turned to the pastor of my church—really out of desperation. And he was the right person to turn to. He let me know that I didn't have to figure anything out—that there were ways to find comfort even in the 'not knowing' state I was in about Kate. He did this not by preaching at me, or ladling on advice—but by listening. And even sharing a similar experience he'd undergone in his own family. But it was his total lack of judgmentalism and his serenity that made it safe for me. I don't know if I'll ever be able to connect with Kate again, but with the help of this pastor, I've been able to live with the uncertainty."

Don't dismiss members of the clergy before you've given one a chance to listen. There's more help here than you may know.

When Alcohol or Drugs Are Involved:
The Wisdom of Twelve-Step Programs

Not all family estrangements are alcohol- or drug-related, but many are. In my own family, while I wouldn't call any member "alcoholic," alcohol has nonetheless fueled some stormy cocktail hours and loosened tongues in very destructive ways. Whether or not any of my family members are alcoholic, I have, however, been greatly helped by attending Al-Anon meetings, a self-help group for people who are struggling to extricate themselves from the bonds of other people's addictive behaviors.

Al-Anon's considerable power comes from helping people who love alcoholics and drug addicts to understand the disease from which their loved ones suffer—and to "keep the focus on themselves" as they do it: to recognize the limits of their influence. The lesson applies to the rest of us, too—especially in the wake of a family cutoff. The behavior of families who reject and disown relatives is always similar to the maneuvering that goes on in alcoholic families. Not only Al-Anon but ACOA (Adult Children of Alcoholics) and CODA (Co-dependents Anonymous) all have free meetings throughout the world and offer an excellent source of support for anyone going through the crisis of family estrangement.

Indeed, virtually every survivor of a family cutoff I've talked to shares a central feature with people who are trying to extricate themselves from dysfunctional behaviors with alcoholics: the struggle to feel that we deserve better treatment from our families than we are getting. Whether it's an unwillingness to tolerate abuse, to apologize for crimes which were never committed, or refusal to comply with outrageous and inappropriate demands, there is often commonality here—realizing that abusive treatment is no longer tolerable.

Deborah started going regularly to Al-Anon meetings right after her parents refused to be involved in her wedding to her fiancé Jacques because he is African-American. "I always knew Dad drank too much, and I always thought my mother was ridiculously wimpy for putting up with it. What I had never realized, though, was how in so many ways I've accommodated my dad just as fearfully—and probably out of the same motive, not wanting to rile him up, not wanting to suffer his verbal abuse when he's drunk. Al-Anon has helped me so much to see not only that his disease is not mine, and even to have some compassion for whatever demons are in him, but it reinforces that I don't have to put up with it—and I'm not somehow a 'bad daughter' for upsetting him. When I got the courage to talk in an Al-Anon meeting and tell my story, the support I felt was unbelievable. I wasn't alone—that was clear. It really helped me to gain perspective not only about my family, but about my own right to choose and chart my own path with Jacques. I honestly don't know if I would have survived that time without the love and support of those amazing people."

Other Sources for Venting and Getting Loving Support

The Internet is full of resources, information, and support groups of all kinds. The digital revolution has provided answers to chronic problems of cost and lack of anonymity in the treatment of mental health. Even though the general state of mental health care still needs vast improvement, the landscape of therapeutic options on the Internet has in many ways radically altered in favor of the consumer.

The National Mental Health Association located in Alexandria, Virginia, can provide information about local self-help groups and community clinics.

You can access them on the World Wide Web at www.nmha.org or reach them via phone at 1-800-969-NMHA.

It may seem disingenuous to suggest finding a therapist to provide that needed caring but dispassionate ear: obviously, this is a route I would encourage you to take. Not perhaps to the exclusion of other ears we've investigated here, but it's very likely during this triage period that you'll benefit greatly from someone trained to help you to overcome the worst symptoms of acute stress syndrome—from which virtually every family rift survivor suffers to some degree. Finding a good therapist is an art in itself—but in addition to querying local mental health organizations (or the above NMHA organization) for suggestions, query your friends who are happy with the therapy they may be pursuing. A professional ear may be exactly what you need right now.

Three Talk Tools for Trauma Recovery

Talk *productively*. Yes, talk until you're blue in the face. But if you find you're running through the same openings in the same maze over and over again (and getting to the same dead-end), you may want to consider the following suggestions, even now, at your venting stage. You'll benefit from these productive talking tips as you go on even more, but it's not a bad idea to cast an eye over them at the start. They'll eventually help you to get out of the maze and into the wider avenues of a new and happier life.

1. Universalize

David, a fifty-three-year-old civil engineer, came to see me after one of his grown sons suddenly stopped returning his phone calls and seemingly had broken off all contact. "I just couldn't calm down, sleep at night—I can barely eat. I can't even think of anything else at this point," David muttered. "Craig and I have always had some difficulties with each other, but we've always managed to have a relationship. I know he's not wild about my wife, Marie, and always, quite erroneously, believed that she was the cause of his mother's and my divorce. But that was many years ago. When Marie and I had our son, Craig was already out of college and engaged and ready to start his own family. He wasn't thrilled about me having another child, and he let me know this by his lack of enthusiasm and support for us when the baby was born. Now, eight years later, he simply refuses to acknowledge my wife, his eight-year-old half-brother, or me. It's turned me into a lunatic. I just can't get a hold of it—sometimes I feel like I'm losing my mind!"

Not knowing the reasons for the cutoff by Craig has made David feel he was going insane. Craig had, in effect, deprived David of any framework within which he might begin to understand how to reach his son and heal the rift. In fact, David was having a completely natural reaction given the circumstances. Reassuring him of this amounts to universalizing his distress—helping him to see that anyone facing a similar dilemma would be likely to feel exactly the same way. But universalizing means something more: not only reassuring David about his sanity, but that his extreme phase of distress *would pass*. Sometimes simply hearing this can be of more healing benefit than anything else: "It will pass."

2. *Partialize the Task*

One of the most important lessons I know to pass on to therapy patients, whatever the presenting problem they bring to me may be, is that trying to tackle the entirety of a problem big enough to bring them into therapy is virtually a sure setup for defeat. One of the best tools to help you contend with any profound interpersonal difficulty is to partialize your task: break it down into manageable components.

Right now you're tackling symptoms of shock and devastation—and trying to recover enough to function and get to a place where you can begin to strategize to make your life better, and achieve some kind of perspective about the family rift you've undergone. You have to get yourself back in working order, and this means attending to basics: talking, eating, sleeping, seeking support from appropriate sources, employing soothing psychological band-aids, if they help to calm you down. Think of how you would treat a battered child: this is how you must treat yourself. This is not the time to decide to switch careers, turn yourself overnight into a new person, or otherwise make sweeping long-term changes in your life.

Recall Lori whom we met earlier—whose mother and sister had kidnapped her son Ryan and somehow convinced Ryan's psychiatrist that she was an unfit mother. At first, Lori's only thought was how she'd fight them in court. She obsessed over what she'd say, what strategies she'd work out with her lawyer—

she had imagined it up to the Supreme Court within hours of hearing what had happened. She was even more of an emotional wreck as a result. She first needed to recover from the shock and feelings of total abandonment by her biological family as simply and honestly as she could bear: this was *not* the time to go flying into court. It was the time to recover from shock—through the means we've been exploring throughout this chapter. Staying alive and functioning well in basic ways (getting up, going to work, taking physical care of herself, reaching out to talk to others) was all she could do right now—and it was a lot.

Everything else had to wait while she fought for her own life and sanity. Only then could she make effective moves toward getting her son Ryan back, and seeking to heal the terrible rift between her and her mother and sister.

3. Avoid Catastrophizing

Dan came to me for therapy just before his law school graduation because of what seemed to be an insurmountable problem with his parents. "My parents have never really gotten along, but in the past few years it's gotten intolerable. They've separated—and will probably divorce. My mom has moved on in her life—but my dad just sits in his own resentments. Any show of support I give her, he registers as an insult to him—I'm really between a rock and a hard place now. Since they've essentially cut each other off from each other, I don't know what to do about graduation. It was hard getting through law school and I'm proud of it, and want both my parents to be there. My mom is willing to come even if my dad is there, as long as they stay apart, but my father refuses to come if my mom will be there—and rubs it in by saying he was the one who paid for law school, therefore I should 'choose' him. He's on the verge of cutting me off, too. It's gotten to the point where I don't want to go to my own graduation. Everything seems so bleak. I feel like my world is coming to an end."

It's not unusual to feel like you're in a complete emotional catastrophe in a situation like Dan describes. "Everything seems so bleak" is an understatement: when a major event takes place under conditions of this degree of family enmity, the whole universe can seem like it's imploding in on you. However, the temptation to view things in the kind of bleak, black-and-white way that Dan has given into here is something we can and should resist.

Dan is "catastrophizing"—extrapolating from an admittedly painful parental tug-of-war to an overriding sense of doom that isn't warranted. Reality is always more modulated than we think; the situation is never as bad as the catastrophizer perceives. I reminded Dan that he was a bright guy with a stellar law school average, and his father really wasn't so powerful that he could stop him from getting a good job in a city as large as New York—a catastrophe of paranoia which Dan had gotten to the verge of entertaining. Dan's prospects for the future were fine; he had many close friends who would be at the graduation to support him. Nothing was as dire as he thought it was.

The point here isn't to convince Dan not to have his feelings—but to remind Dan that he had more of a choice than he realized not to go off the handle and expand those feelings into a hurricane of despair. Reality is softer and more rounded than we think—even at the point of despair and hurt and anger we feel from a family rift.

Time for a Deep Breath

Acknowledging trauma takes care and an abundance of self-compassion. But as you've seen in the breakdown of this first crucial step, healing is possible almost immediately—if you stay honest, find appropriate ears to share what you're feeling, and keep it very simple. Being in shock is no fun. You can't be too gentle with yourself.

Honesty and gentleness pay off. They will help you to begin the ascent to healing that our next step will make even more accessible.

2

Start to Live, Laugh, and Be Happy
Now: Taking Back Your Life

After all I've said about how long it takes to heal from the effects of a family rift, this step's encouragement to "live, laugh, and be happy" may strike you as contradictory, maybe even perverse. Am I suddenly suggesting that you *can*, after all, shrug it off and go on as if nothing unpleasant were happening?

Not at all. However, I *am* suggesting—in fact, promising—that you have resources you may not realize you have to "get back in the saddle" of your life. Finding and employing these resources will take courage, but not courage to pretend that things are better. It's the courage to take what steps you can to regain enough balance to proceed through your days with equanimity—even sometimes with pleasure. And now, after the hard first look you've just taken at the effects of the trauma you've just gone through, is the crucial time to go about finding and using whatever tactics are available to you to get your life back.

Think of it this way: you've shoved back the drapes, opened the window, and sunlight has now filled the room. Yes, it lights up the mess—but, with the support you've already reached out for to help you to begin to *look* at that mess, you'll find you can focus on something else, too. You can lift your eyes up from the wreckage for a moment, and look out through the newly opened window into the sunlit sky. Imagine feeling its light and warmth on your face, and its reassurance in your heart—its reminder that you are still fully alive, here, breathing, capable, the most important parts of your life and capacities still intact.

Building a Bridge Back to Life

Let's look at how you can find and bolster this inner sense of aliveness—and not only learn to go on, but even sometimes thrive, right now, in the context of even the most painful challenges you're facing. This is crucial for another reason: the sturdier and more reliable a sense of personal well-being you can foster in yourself right now, the more probing, illuminating, and helpful will be your further discoveries about your family rift. You can't climb a mountain or go on a safari if you're not appropriately equipped.

Reclaiming your life—and the realization that you still can be happy, even now—is a part of the essential equipment for your "trip," all in service of what many twelve-step programs call building "a bridge back to life." You might want to keep in mind another axiom of which these support groups also make very powerful use: right actions lead to right thinking, rarely the other way around. And the right actions you need to take right now amount to anything that will reawaken you to your capacity for joy—and bring a measure of it back into your life.

Right Actions Leading to Right Thinking
- Rediscover your autonomy
- Value who you are—right now
- Personal entitlement: what you have the right to expect
- The power of gratitude
- Honoring your obligations

You'll see, as we review each of these one by one that, like every other step and tactic we'll employ in these pages, these admonitions hold some surprises.

Rediscover Your Autonomy

We've seen that shame is an inevitable part of the mix of feelings you must deal with now. If you've undergone a family cutoff, you know this, especially after looking it in the face in the first step we've just explored. Even if you perceive yourself as sinned-against, you very likely feel the shame of belonging to a family in which this kind of psychic violence—ultimatums, physical or emotional abuse, or however the rift has manifested for you—is even possible. However, since few family splits proceed from pure good guy versus bad guy scenarios, it's even more likely that you feel some sense of shared responsibility for what's happened. "If only they hadn't" can mix with "If only *I* hadn't" in a mind-numbing dance. Sometimes the "If only I hadn'ts" begin to crowd out the "If only they hadn'ts": self-blaming—and the shame of feeling that the family break is all your fault—may rise up in you like toxic magma.

Now isn't the time to worry about whether you or "they" are right or wrong, however. We're still setting the stage for the deeper investigations you'll be making in the rest of this book, doing what we can to get you ready to make those explorations as profitable as they can be. And that means learning to lighten up on yourself. Even when you seem hell-bent on being miserable—and taking the blame for it all.

Shame—and the self-attacks and recriminations it breeds—probably comprise the single most powerful impediment to learning to do this. According to psychologist Eric Erikson, a child experiences shame when his or her autonomy is thwarted. Shame and doubt flood anyone who feels dependent: not believing you have the wherewithal to take care of yourself, you will always feel prey to—weaker than—those whom you perceive are calling the shots. Unfortunately, because this usually happens so early in childhood, you may have only a dim sense of this. And it's often exacerbated on the occasion of a family rift: all those "it's my fault" feelings typically come rushing back.

The good news is that a family rift may actually give you an unprecedented opportunity finally to begin to separate healthily and individuate (become your own person) from a family and family assumptions that once stifled you. In David's case, the trigger for realizing this was, on the face of it, absurdly trivial: ordering a pizza.

Recall David's shock at his son Craig turning his back on him. "I really didn't feel I'd done anything wrong—but I couldn't get over feeling as if I had. I felt terrible feelings of guilt and shame about it—that somehow I'd been a lousy father, and David cutting me off was the proof. There was the divorce—and sure, I know Craig had been very understandably upset about that. No kid likes to see his parents break up. But I'd done everything I could to make Craig comfortable around my new wife Marie, and he just wasn't having any of it. Marie kept reassuring me that whatever had happened wasn't my fault, but I just couldn't get this sick feeling out of my gut that it was."

What David had slowly begun to realize in the course of acknowledging the trauma of "losing" his son was that these feelings weren't new. "When I was a kid, and my own father shut down at home, I remember also feeling it was my fault—even though, logically, I couldn't figure out why. And here I was feeling the same way with Craig."

Marie, allying with her husband and attempting to talk him out of feeling that he'd caused it but getting nowhere, had begun to lose patience with him. "It wasn't just that I couldn't jolt him out of this self-blaming rut," she says. "He'd started to shut down with me, too. It was like he felt emasculated by this rift—it just proved what an incompetent jerk he was. He felt he couldn't do anything right. I couldn't stand his pain—but I was also getting tired of my own. He just kept shutting me out and our marriage was going down the tubes." Marie, normally very even-tempered—"more of a peace-keeper even than David, usually"—uncharacteristically blew her top at him.

"She literally shook me by the shoulders. I'm a pretty big guy and she's about five-foot-one, so this was a surprise to both of us," David said. "She pleaded with me to wake up to the fact that I had been a very good husband to her, and a good father to Craig. Why couldn't I see that? She told me I was ignoring her—this was ruining our marriage, she said, and we just had to do something about it quick."

David closed his eyes for a moment, and rubbed his forehead. Then he continued, quietly: "She was right. I can still see her hurt, enraged face. I'd never seen her look like that. She began to cry—something she never did. And—somehow—it was like a reflex—I softened inside, began to make contact with how much I loved her, and put my arms around her. It felt unfamiliar. I realized I hadn't just held her, gently, reassuringly—like the husband I used to be—in so long. Somehow in that embrace, some sense of my own— power, I guess—self-worth, maybe—came back to me. I felt a new sense of release as I held my wife in my arms and realized once again that she loved me and I loved her. Like I said, something in me softened. And yet the outcome was, I felt stronger. Less besieged by myself."

David continued: "I'm not saying hugging Marie 'cured' me. I'm still distraught about Craig. How could I not be? I still have doubts about how good a father I've been to him. But I realized I had put a lot of energy into my life *now*—my life with Marie—and I wasn't the incompetent bum that some tape in my head had been telling me I was." This felt, David said, "like the first true moment of self-acceptance I'd experienced since—God knows when. Maybe since Craig stopped talking to me. I don't know. All I know is, feeling her melt in my arms for the first time in so long, I felt so grateful to her and for the life we'd built together. Then, out of nowhere, her tears subsiding, she suddenly looked brightly up into my face as if I'd finally turned back into her best friend and boyfriend. 'Wanna get a pizza?' she asked me."

David laughs. "When she made that suggestion, like a sixteen-year-old, I realized something very special. I had a good life. Whatever was going wrong with Craig, *I had a good life*. And I deserved it. I didn't feel, I guess, so dependent on my son's approval of me anymore. I didn't feel dependent on anyone's approval."

What David describes is not so much a renewed sense of self-worth as a renewed sense of autonomous *self*. Somehow after Marie's uncharacteristically angry, pleading outburst—and as the product of finding that he could reach out to reassure *her* for a change ("she'd been doing all the reassuring up till now," he says)—he was able to feel stronger and freer. He had power again.

This isn't to suggest that his shame, or anyone else's shame similarly rooted deep in childhood, can be magically banished in a single stroke. However, David has discovered that he can nudge himself out of the rut of shameful self-blaming by paying attention to the full life he's developed, himself, on his own—the life he now had with Marie. Much remained to be faced about his rift with Craig—but now, as David put it, "getting a pizza was the first right thing to do. I realized in that moment I could normalize a lot of my life. I could still *enjoy* things. I wasn't a bum. I had power to change my reactions. I didn't have to knuckle under to the pain of feeling I'd lost my son."

Value Who You Are—Right Now

David's recognition is a powerful one. It depended on something simple, although usually tough to allow yourself: becoming vulnerable, opening up to receive what other people you trust have to say about you that you cannot see. That Marie was ready to help David understand he wasn't the "bum" he'd long been telling himself he was, underscores something important. You need to find people who can reliably reflect back to you who you really are, because right now, on your own, it's very unlikely that you're able to see yourself with any clarity. You can't, in other words, do this alone. This "reflection" often happens in therapy, with a friend or friends, in support groups—but sometimes in wholly unpredictable contexts.

Lori, who was devastated when her mother and sister kidnapped her son, accusing her of being an unfit mother, found her way to an awakening in some ways similar to David's. However, Lori's route to this awakening led her to see what she hadn't seen about herself in much more detail—and in a group she never imagined in her life she'd end up joining.

"It happened," Lori said, "in a women's reading group a friend of mine at work invited me to join. Cheryl knew something of what I'd been through, and she was a good friend—wanted to think up things she could help me do to get out of myself. After my son was taken away, I just about collapsed. I could barely drag myself to work. I looked awful—didn't care what I threw on as clothes. I used to care so much about what I wore! Somehow I managed to function at work—during that time most of what I had to do was rote, thank heavens. I don't know what I would've done if I'd had to actually *think*. But Cheryl kept calling me—wouldn't leave me alone—and it was good she kept at me. Because if she hadn't, I think I might've just gone home one day and never come out again."

Not that Lori was especially eager to talk about books with a bunch of other women. "Like I said, I didn't want to have to think about anything. I just wanted to shut down. But somehow I knew not to—maybe I could just go to this group and sit in the back and drink tea and, I don't know, get something out of actually being with people who weren't trying to lock me up." There were eight women in the group, who ranged in age from twenty-six to seventy-eight. "The oldest woman, Gracie, was the leader of it. We met in her house. It was nice, early American, a fireplace, cookies and tea. I liked being there. Gracie talked a lot but she wasn't obnoxious. She was sweet, and smart. She really seemed to care about reading and getting the group to care about it too. I think she'd been a high school teacher once. Anyway, they'd been reading some novel on the bestseller list I hadn't even heard of, and that nobody liked. I was just there to get acquainted, so I wasn't expected to contribute—which was fine with me. Everyone was disgusted with this book, though—too much violence and sex. Gracie had an idea. 'Let's read something tried and true. Something none of us has read in a long time. Like *The Old Man and the Sea*.'"

It was late, the cookies were gone, and the women's group was clearly ready to disperse—so everyone agreed quickly. Lori and Cheryl talked on the way home about the group—and about whether Lori wanted to continue in it. Lori still felt listless—but at Cheryl's urging, she agreed to come at least once more. "At least I saw the movie of that book," Lori told Cheryl. "Spencer Tracy, right?"

Cheryl encouraged Lori to read the book again—she'd feel more a part of things. "I'm no literary whiz," Lori said to me afterwards, "and this all sounded like a high school homework assignment—up to and including Gracie acting as teacher. I couldn't imagine having anything to contribute. But I was at a point when I was just taking suggestions almost without thinking, and I seemed to remember the book wasn't long, so I agreed to take it out of the library and read it."

Lori was right—the book wasn't long. But she hadn't counted on its effect on her. "I wasn't expecting to be so moved. This old guy no one thought anything about—I mean, it was such a simple story, but the fact that his pain and struggle and triumph and then loss of the one thing he'd struggled so hard to get, this huge marlin—the fact that all this happened to him with no one else ever knowing about it. I can't tell you—it sank down to the center of me. So much of my own pain and struggle in my life, competing with my sister, feeling so disapproved of by my parents—all of my real feelings, anything I cared about—I somehow realized, reading this little Hemingway book, I'd gone through totally alone. And yet this old man somehow was transformed by what he'd gone through. He wasn't miserable or destroyed by the amazing adventure nobody but he knew he had. He was changed by it. Fulfilled."

Lori surprised herself at the next meeting by being the first woman to raise her hand and saying pretty much what I've quoted her as saying here. "I remember Gracie being completely quiet while I went on about the book. I guess what I said struck a chord. I don't know. But after I was done, she looked at me really hard, hard but with a lot of compassion, even love. And she said, 'You know what he went through, don't you.' And I felt tears well up, but also the first smile I'd felt on my face since my boy was taken from me. 'Yeah, I do,' I said. Cheryl was sitting next to me, and reached for my hand. I felt I'd actually rejoined the human race."

When Lori woke up the next morning she was aware of having changed somehow inside. She chose her clothes with more care. She even put on a necklace—something she hadn't had the least desire to wear since her son Ryan was taken from her. (Remember her dream about beads and her mother's bead factory.) "I picked up the crystal necklace, feeling a little bewildered," Lori said. "Why did I suddenly care what I looked like? Why was I feeling— better? My family was still treating me terribly—I still had the ordeal of the court custody case ahead of me—but I didn't feel like I was hauling lead any- more. I felt lighter, even happy. I looked at myself in the mirror and some- thing of the woman I'd once been before all this had happened—something came back."

Lori's appearance drew surprised acclaim at work—and especially from Cheryl. In the weeks that followed, she found herself able to do things she hadn't done in many months: "I went to the movies with another friend. I went out to lunch with my colleagues at work. I kept going back to Gracie's book group. I cleaned up my apartment—started paying more attention to my life. But the main thing was, I couldn't get that triumph and feeling of completion that I'd encountered in *The Old Man and the Sea* out of my mind. Somehow that made me start to value myself again."

Valuing herself wasn't something Lori had ever been encouraged to do as a child. But when she brought this up herself, I had an idea. I asked her what traits she might check off on a list of them I had once offered her as part of a self-esteem workshop she attended. "Oh God," she said. "I remember that list all right. I think I was able to pick out two traits I thought applied to me. 'Consistent' and 'discreet.'" Lori laughed loudly at herself. "You know," she said, smiling, "I think I might just pick out a few more if I saw that list again."

The list is long, but I've found it to be a very interesting barometer of how people feel about themselves—especially when they compare the traits they check off at different times. Lori was right about seeing more on the list that applied to her than she'd seen before. Of the thirty-five traits listed, Lori was amazed to find she felt thirty of them ("maybe thirty-one") now applied to her. Look at the list below. Circle or jot down the traits you feel apply to you. Make a copy and keep it with you so you can draw strength from it when you're feeling low. Ask your best friend or your partner or someone else who loves you to tell you if you're leaving out any qualities that you need to work on integrating here.

My Inner Net Worth Qualities

- Friendly
- Generous
- Competent
- Creative
- Persevering
- Resourceful
- Artistic
- Strong
- Stylish
- Imaginative
- Sexy
- Funny
- A Good lover
- Consistent
- A good friend
- Expressive
- Disciplined
- Devoted to my family
- A fun person to be around
- Whimsical
- Entertaining
- A good conversationalist
- Able to handle crisis
- Warm
- Sensitive
- Charming
- Empathetic
- Discreet
- Good-natured
- Easy-going
- Compassionate
- Healthy
- Physically fit
- Determined
- Charming

Can you guess the thirty ("maybe thirty-one") Lori chose? All she'll tell you now, smiling, is, "It's a big change from two."

Personal Entitlement: What You Have the Right to Expect

What grows from the kinds of "aha!" moments we've seen David and Lori reach in their separate ways is the stronger sense not only that you already have more power to find and create happiness in your life, no matter how dire the circumstances of your family rift may seem to you, but that you have a *right* to happiness—now. We've touched on Erikson's suggestion that shame— reflexive shame that won't go away—always has early roots in childhood, and that it is importantly the product of feeling your autonomy has been compromised or blocked. Few victims of a family rift haven't undergone this wound.

You already have more than an inkling that the eruption of your family "volcano" was preceded by years—lifetimes—of rising toxic heat. Explosions don't come from nowhere. And part of that rising toxicity is bound up in the crippling sense, inevitable in children whose sense of self has been caged and impeded the way most family rift victims have felt blocked, that you don't deserve "autonomy." That it's presumptuous to think you'd be able to exist without the strictures and judgments to which your family has subjected you. More seriously, you grow up not having any idea of what is *appropriate* to expect—what you have the *right* to expect—from yourself and from other people, even after you leave the family fold.

Self-esteem is a phrase bandied about so universally that we're often numb to its meaning. "Oh, she has low self-esteem." "He ought to feel better about himself." "Why is she always dragging herself down? She should snap out of it." The problem with these assessments of others is that they don't address the central wound of people who feel bad about themselves. These assessments don't proceed from the understanding that those with "low self-esteem" don't, in their heart, know that there's an alternative.

However much we may, at the prodding of self-help pundits and magazine self-assessment questionnaires ("How to Learn to Love Yourself in Ten Easy Steps"), attempt to white-knuckle ourselves out of low self-esteem, we don't appreciate that most of the deepest judgments we make about ourselves feel to us like immutable truth. It doesn't help to tell someone they *ought* to think differently about themselves if they're already sure they *know* they couldn't be any different. Whether you say the words or not, your response to this sort of well-meant chastising is generally, on some very deep level, "I know I should feel better about myself but I can't." If everyone else knew the "real awful truth" about you, they'd understand how hopeless an endeavor "feeling better about myself" really was.

However, as you learned in our first step, when you allow yourself simply to *see* and acknowledge the trauma of a family rift without instantly trying to change what you see, you begin to awaken to the relativity of your assumptions about the trauma, to the notion not only that they're not inevitable, but that they're susceptible to reinterpretation and change. Now, through the kind of "right" (and deceptively superficial) actions you've seen David and Lori variously felt induced to take (ordering a pizza, reading *The Old Man and the Sea*, putting on a crystal necklace), you've seen how permitting yourself this vulnerable contact with the frightening "tapes" in your head—with the help of others you trust who reflect back to you that you're *not* the pariah those "tapes" keep telling you that you are—will sometimes spontaneously change your behavior, and bring you to more positive feelings and self-views.

We've seen Deborah, whose alcoholic father's racially bigoted condemnation of her fiancé Jacques shut the door on her relationship with her father, begin to see a truer reflection of who she is and what was really going on with the aid of her friends in Al-Anon. This has helped her to understand that her lifelong tactic of backing down and "keeping the peace" had not only crippled her relationship with her father, but had become an impediment in the rest of her life as well. "I didn't realize this," Deborah said, "until, going to Al-Anon, and talking endlessly with Jacques about my childhood, I started for the first time in my life to get angry about how hemmed in I'd always felt."

Deborah lets out a whoosh of a sigh. "Too soft a word. *Rageful.* This latest episode of my father's cruel dismissal of me was certainly the hardest I'd yet had to face, but it was just the last in a series of dismissals I'd gotten from him all through my life. And the classic problem—not being able to get any sort of compensatory attention from my mother, who although she also had to put up with his emotional abuse had long become inured to it, didn't even realize how bad it was—well, I started to get really angry at her, too. Jacques still was my oasis—but I know he was getting tired of every conversation turning into an antifamily tirade."

Al-Anon helped her to get some perspective about this swing of the pendulum from overaccommodation to rageful vengeance—and to have some compassion for the swings. "I realized, listening to other people who'd suffered from similar swings that I didn't know what I was *supposed* to expect from people. I didn't have any clear idea what healthy relationships were supposed to be like. My love for Jacques is so strong that it seems to sort of cover all this pain sometimes, and even gives me the illusion that he can cure that pain, but I've found myself clinging so hard to him, depending so much on him, that he's become wary. He says that a lot of what I want our marriage to 'cure' it can't cure. He's been very gentle, but clear about this: 'This is your stuff, Honey,' he said to me once. 'I'll stay right with you, but I can't wave some magic wand and make it all better.' That was on the mark. I really did want him somehow to magically make it all go away. Luckily, in Al-Anon, I heard enough people talk about similar cravings to escape pain through some magical quick-fix to see that I was trying to do the same thing. And that it wouldn't work."

But knowing there was no quick fix was not enough. Deborah had to learn some basics about what she was entitled to expect from other people in relationships. Lists of positive assumptions or traits (like the Inner Net Worth Qualities list you read above as part of Lori's continuing story) are not, on their own, generally much help: they can just reinforce how badly you feel about yourself. How "you wish you could change but you just can't." However, the right words at the right time can do wonders. For example, Deborah had done the work of acknowledging the pain her father's rejection had caused her, understanding through the reflective help of Jacques and her Al-Anon friends that her pain was in fact *her* pain—something only she could address. Because of this, she was more receptive than she would otherwise have been to registering the surprising truths of the following Personal Bill of Rights.

The degree of shock you may find yourself feeling as you allow these rights into your heart and mind ("you mean I really have the right to say what I please?") is a gift: it gives you a red flag about what most needs attention. And any attempt to normalize your life right now—to find pleasure again in your day-to-day activities, and develop a more rooted sense of well-being—depends on heeding those red flags. I strongly suggest that you look at this list frequently. Its psychic map will help you find your way back to higher ground when, for the moment, your emotional storms obscure your understanding of what you really are entitled to enjoy, in every aspect of your life.

Your Personal Bill of Rights
- The right to feel good about who I am
- The freedom to say what I please and the wisdom to know when to say it
- The freedom to protect myself in a responsible and mature manner
- The right to ask for what I want, and the wisdom to know where and whom to ask
- The right to exercise my innate creative abilities
- The freedom to say no to a family member when dictated by my best interest
- The right to respectful and dignified treatment
- The right to know who I am
- The freedom to know what I want
- The right to choose the life I want
- The right to assert my likes and dislikes

- The right to accept myself for who I am
- The freedom to regulate my thoughts and feelings without the input of another person
- The freedom to cultivate interests and points of view
- The right to tolerate points of view that differ from mine
- The ability to accommodate another person without losing my own identity
- The freedom to assert my rights without fear of loss of love
- The freedom to assert my rights without fear of rejection and abandonment
- The freedom to assert my rights without fear of physical or mental punishment
- The right to say no
- The right to feel alive
- The right to believe that I am likable
- The right to make choices in my life
- The freedom to choose my own friends
- The right to set boundaries that will be respected
- The right to follow my own interests

Deborah's anger at not feeling she had the right to expect most of these entitlements can still flare up alarmingly. "But reviewing this list now, over time, has begun to calm me down more than rile me up about what I don't get from other people. More than that, it's helped me to be appropriately assertive in all my relationships—as well as to give others, Jacques especially, the kind of respect I know now *I* have the right—am entitled—to receive from people. And when I don't get the treatment this list tells me I deserve, at the very least I know it's not my fault. I have a clearer idea of what a good life is supposed to be. And now I even think I might be able to live it—whatever happens between my father and me, I don't have to put up with abuse. That may seem obvious to anyone else, but it's a revelation to me."

The Power of Gratitude

When you've begun to see how many avenues are still open to you for happiness—when you've begun to take action, as Lori put it, to "rejoin the human race"—something quite startling happens. After months or years of feeling that there was no exit from the hurt and depression and anger and terror caused by your family rift, the sun breaks through the clouds for a moment and you catch yourself feeling something very odd. This may be very fleeting at first—an unaccustomed moment of peace, of enjoying who you are and what you're doing and whom you're doing it with. But it's a feeling to take note of. It's the glimmer of a shift in your attitude, in your awareness— and it's something to feel grateful for. Not only at the moment you feel it, but to take note of for future reference.

Twelve-step programs often encourage their members to write, keep, and consult a gratitude list—a list of what they're thankful for in their lives. However, many twelve-step members first dig in their heels at the thought. Once again, a list of even the most positive words generally has little force on its own, and can even make you feel worse, if that list strikes you as something you're supposed to feel but don't. However, even if you don't feel like doing it—even if it seems like some silly fourth grade homework assignment—making a gratitude list can turn out to be incredibly helpful, if not right at the moment you first itemize it, then later on. As with Lori's surprise at returning to her list of Inner Net Worth Qualities, you will probably be very struck by how important the items on that gratitude list turn out to be when you look at it a couple days afterward. You'll also probably find yourself adding to the list as you let go of your resistance to accepting what's on it. The abundance of life is so much greater than we start out knowing in the wake of a family rift trauma. Keeping a gratitude list can help you keep track of some of that welcome abundance.

Jack, a recovering alcoholic who's been sober for ten years, was one AA-member who first groaned at the thought of a gratitude list. "I was so upset about Kyle, my son, whom I'd finally had to turn out of the house because he smoked crack, and was turning our lives into a nightmare. I was upset about the pain I knew he was in—but also because, until ten years ago when I stopped drinking and taking drugs, he'd had to put up with a nightmare from me. I can't help feeling responsible for how he's turned out. It's been the hardest thing for me to face in my life. I value my own sobriety right now above anything else—but this stab in my heart about Kyle just keeps me from feeling 'happy, joyous, and free'—which AA keeps telling me I will feel if I just give myself time and take the right actions. Well, I've given myself time, and I'm doing what I know how to do, but I still feel this awful weight in my heart."

The possible benefits of making a gratitude list finally occurred to Jack recently when Sally, one of his other three children ("They're all younger than Kyle, and none of them had to put up with my shenanigans when I was drinking and drugging, so at least I feel I didn't make it harder than I had to for them") came home from her first grade class, crying, with a small bump on her head. She ran into her daddy's arms. "Billy threw his lunchbox at me!" she whimpered.

"I'd had an awful day at work, none of the vendors I dealt with at the shipping plant I manage had delivered supplies we'd ordered on time. My wife was away visiting her ailing mother, so I had all three kids to take care of, once the babysitter left after I got home. I just wasn't in the mood to deal with Sally's bump on the head—which I could see wasn't that bad to begin with. At first I tried to keep from sounding as impatient with her as I felt ('Don't cry, Honey, it's not that bad'), but she was very upset and wouldn't stop wailing. I just didn't have the patience for it.

"Suddenly I grabbed her and stood her up on her feet in front of me and yelled at her to stop being such a baby. The look on her face—and how she winced when she heard me yell—oh God, it stopped me in my tracks. I thought of how I'd abused everyone in my life before I got sober. I thought of how often I'd yelled at Kyle when I was drunk—just like I was yelling at Sally now. It was unbearable. I took her into my arms—she still was so stiff and afraid, whimpering—and I did all I could to calm her down, holding her, apologizing for shouting at her, letting her know it would all be all right. She calmed down soon, and the storm passed. But this sudden capacity to really hear and feel for Sally, to stop yelling and apologize, left a kind of golden feeling in me.

"I realized in that instant how grateful I was to be there, to be a father who could be available to his kids, so grateful for the home and wife and life I'd been able to create in sobriety. The notion of keeping a gratitude list didn't seem so impossible now. In fact, I let Sally help me. 'Get me that pad and pencil over on the table, Honey,' I told her. She did. 'Are we gonna draw pictures?' she asked me hopefully. And I thought, yeah, actually, although I'd planned to write words on the list of what made me thankful, drawing pictures of it seemed like an even better idea, especially because Sally could help me.

"So she climbed on my lap while I held the pencil over the paper. And I told her I was going to draw a picture of her, because I wanted to draw pictures of all the things I loved most. I'm no artist—it was a stick figure with curls—but she was delighted. Then she took the pencil and drew a picture of the house. Then I took it back and drew a big plate of spaghetti. We went on until the paper was covered with all the things I now knew were gifts—gifts that filled me with an unbelievable joy. A roof over my head, enough food to eat, my children, my wife, our SUV, the kids' toys—well, let's just say it's a 'list' of drawings I look at every day since it's now held up by a magnet on the refrigerator door. And it grounds me. Reminds me how amazing my life has become."

What will happen between Kyle and Jack has yet to play out. "I feel stronger about letting Kyle find his own way—and I beat myself up less for having failed him when he was the age Sally is now. Funny how beating myself up less has freed me to love him more. Which means feel pain for what he's going through, but with the stronger sense that I'm doing all I can now to be there for him—and everyone else in my life—when and if they need me."

Gratitude lists help ground me, too. When I was getting ready for my son Kenny's bar mitzvah, contending with all my upsetting feelings about the fact that his grandparents—my father and mother—wouldn't be attending threw me sometimes into a terrible depression. That I was able to focus on what I was grateful for even at these moments of deep funk is a testament to having trained myself to do it before when I'd felt bad. I learned over time that taking the action of writing down what I love in my life, what I'm thankful for, is always at least potentially a powerfully healing thing to do, especially at moments when I can't feel grateful any other way. Seeing the items on my gratitude list nudges me to a different much more welcome awareness. Here's the list I came up with on that day:

My Gratitude List
- My strength and stamina
- My wonderful wife—beautiful, strong, loving, loyal
- My four terrific children—each a unique gift from the Creator
- A career that I love
- My dogs and cat who always love me, no matter what
- Great friends
- My good health and the good health of my wife and children
- My financial comfort
- My sense of humor
- My ability to give back to the world

- My ability to help myself
- My capacity to express myself
- A great sense of humor and, more important, an ability to laugh at myself

It helps to look at this list, even now. Adding to it helps me too, as I always do, as I go on in my life—and especially at moments when the rift between me and my family fills me with old terrors, self-loathing, and despair. A gratitude list is one of the best ways I know of reminding you how life is always better than it looks at those dark times.

Honoring Your Obligations

So much of building that bridge back to life depends on creating and adhering to a structure, a strategy of daily living that will keep you in contact with people and give some useful and satisfying shape to your days. Lori dragged herself to work even before she had her *Old Man and the Sea* awakening partly because she knew that going to her job, miserable as she was, at least kept her tethered to the outside world. For the same reasons, she followed her friend Cheryl's suggestions because doing so kept her connected at a time when she knew she needed contact with life, even if she couldn't yet summon up any enthusiasm for it. Without some satisfying experience of connection, we're lost, especially when the primal connections in our lives on which we used to depend—our families—feel severed.

"Honoring your obligations" is the phrase I choose to suggest ways—and attitudes—you most profitably bring to creating this all-important connection to life. The operative word is "honoring." It suggests that whatever keeps the avenues open in your life—whether it's work, friends, taking care of your kids, school—deserves to be respected and cultivated. Behaving in a way that you know will serve you—even if you don't feel like carrying the behavior out—always turns out to be healing. The discipline you're able to exert over your behavior right now will save you from emotional storms—giving you a "place" to be—just as a well-built house will protect you from being unnecessarily buffeted by the cold and rain.

This is a lesson Jason and Oliver learned deeply. After Jason's family's wholesale rejection of him for announcing not only that he was gay, but that he was planning a commitment ceremony with his partner Oliver, Jason said he came to a grinding halt. "All the plans we'd made for the ceremony and the reception—the lists of people to invite, the caterer, the trip we were going to take afterwards—all of that suddenly seemed like more than I could ever get done. No, it was worse than that. I think on some level I had absorbed my family's disgust about us—I wouldn't have been able to acknowledge this back then—but now I know that some vestige of the hateful homophobia gripping my family also afflicted me. I started seeing Oliver differently. Did I really want to spend the rest of my life with him? Wasn't this commitment ceremony a mockery of straight marriage? Some attempt to assimilate—to be like 'them'? I got very sour and very cynical.

"And I kicked myself for my timing. I mean, if I hadn't been such a jerk, I could have handled telling my family differently. Dropping the bomb on them that I was going to get 'married' to a man at the same time I told them I was gay—well, what did I expect? I really was on the verge of calling the whole thing off with Oliver. The thing had just been poisoned—all our dreams, all our plans for a life together, just seemed like a lot of sick childish nonsense."

Jason was in this mood when Oliver came home after work one day with the invitations they had had embossed at great expense. "Damn!" Oliver apparently said when he stormed through the door. "They didn't use the font I told them to use! They didn't center the damned text the way I told them to!" Oliver was completely bound up in this upcoming ceremony—even before Jason had "dropped the bomb" on his family, Oliver was the one overseeing all the details. Jason had always enjoyed how much Oliver loved doing it— and was secretly relieved he wouldn't have to deal with flowers and food and font sizes on the invitations himself. But now, in the black mood he was in about the whole deal—Oliver included—he just was disgusted. "Who the hell cares!" he spat out at Oliver—loudly and angrily enough to stop Oliver short.

"Oliver didn't realize I wasn't just in a transitory bad mood," Jason says. "He calmed down, said I was probably right, that the invitations would do just fine. Then he brought out a sheaf of menus he wanted me to see. 'Help me figure out the food, okay?' He was right back bustling on about all the options—'You think a smorgasbord rather than sit-down? I mean, I don't want to be too formal. But the food at the smorgasbord place isn't as good as. . . .'"

Jason's dark mood wasn't budging. It filled the room like a scent. Even Oliver noticed. "What's wrong?" he asked.

Jason decided to tell him. He went on a rampage about how all this was getting out of hand, and it would be too expensive, and they really hadn't thought hard enough about what they were doing or even if they wanted to do it. He grabbed the menus, sent them flying over the couch, slamming into a lamp which fell and broke. The sound of the crash stopped both of them. Jason flumped down deeper into his chair and buried his face in his hands. Oliver was quiet at first. Then he said, "This isn't about us, is it? It's about your folks."

Jason said he sighed deeply and told him he wasn't sure what it was about.

"So it is about us?" Oliver quietly asked. Jason didn't respond. Another long moment of silence, while Oliver got up and retrieved the menus, put the lamp back on the table, carefully took off the broken lampshade. Then he spoke. "Do you love me?"

Jason said he lifted his face from his palms and looked at Oliver. Oliver looked so vulnerable, menus and cracked lampshade falling out of his hands, so open and hurt. And Jason realized something. As deeply as he had registered anything in his life. *Yes*, he did love Oliver. But he knew more than that. He had spent years building a relationship with him. They had ties to each other now. They had both grown to the point of respecting, not just loving, each other. Love, Jason realized at that moment, wasn't just some romantic haze. Love entailed sacrifice, responsibilities—obligations. Obligations he found himself amazed to realize he wanted to carry out—to honor.

"All this sort of shot through my head while I looked at Oliver. I started to cry. He came over to me, held me. And I told him, yes, he was right, it was about my folks—it was like my parents had injected me with some virus by slamming the phone down on me, telling me they never wanted to see me again unless I went 'straight.' Everything had spoiled."

Jason looked out the window at nothing, gathering his thoughts and feelings, before continuing to tell me the story. "But at that moment, looking at Oliver literally trying to stop the breakage and keep it from getting worse, I realized that the important stuff *hadn't* spoiled. It was more important now than ever before that we come through for each other—especially when the family I thought loved me had so summarily cut me off. This wasn't the time to cut ties. It was the time to build on the ones I had. And the one I had with Oliver was the most precious one I knew."

"Honoring obligations" means understanding that what keeps life going—what gives you a realm to live happily. It involves keeping the pacts you've made with people who are important to you. "I realized that without those ties, and the responsibilities they imply, there'd be nothing," Jason said. "Suddenly all the attention to detail Oliver had been lavishing on our ceremony didn't seem like fussiness. Oliver *cared*—and he was showing he cared—in the most direct, concrete ways. He glowed to me as a power of example—something I now knew I wanted to emulate." Jason pauses again. "There's so little that feels safe in my life now. Oliver is a huge part of what gives me a sense of home, the only real feeling of being loved I've got. I now value it more than I ever did to the point of taking the invitations back and making sure the printer got them right this time."

Honoring your obligations also means honoring your obligations to yourself. In fact, that's the primary goal. When we acknowledge, accept, and take full advantage of our interactions with the people we still do have in our lives, and especially when we take steps to bolster the loving connections we have, we help everyone involved—not least ourselves. In this context, you won't think of "honoring obligations" as an onerous chore—even when, like writing that gratitude list when you're miserable, or cleaning up a broken lamp, you may not feel very much like doing it. However, the discipline of carrying it out pays off. You're doing what you can to keep everything that matters in place in your life.

And right now, what matters most, is having as thriving a support system around you as you can. Not just to get you through your day-to-day life at a time when your heart feels like it's been stomped on. But to give you the strength to make the explorations you'll need to make next—that the following steps in this book will enable to you pursue—to heal from the family rift that got you to pick up this book in the first place.

There's a lot more to explore. But by now, happily, you're readier than ever to embark on the trip.

3

Discover Your Family Roles

Now that you've acknowledged the trauma of the family rift and learned that you can begin to find satisfaction in your life even in the fresh wake of that trauma—you're ready to take a closer and more objective look at what's going on in your family than you've been able to do before.

Taking this more cool-headed look is crucial. You can't overcome the effects of a family rift, or begin to investigate how to heal from it, if you don't acquire a clearer sense of the underlying reasons it happened in the first place. We already know the roots of any family rift go deep; now is the time to begin to see how deep they are, where they go, and specifically how they affect you now.

The unnerving news is that most of us have only very dim ideas of these family dynamics; few of us ever thought to question what gave rise to our own family's unique way of interacting. But there's good news, too: when you start to find out what makes your family tick—and explore your own complicity in keeping it ticking—you're on the way to a new liberation. You're en route to discovering you have a range of life-affirming choices in a realm that until now may have seemed like one in which you had few or none at all.

One of the best ways to make this discovery is to look at your family as if it were an ongoing play or film—to see what the larger meaning of the story may be, how the characters in it behave and function in relation to each other, and especially what your own role in the drama is. Here's something you can count on: *every family plays out its own particular drama*. You may not like the plot, nor care very much for many of the leading and supporting roles, but the goal right now doesn't depend on liking or disliking what you make out your family drama to be. The aim here is simply to understand a bit more about the mechanisms that have made the story turn out the way it has. The aim is to achieve clarity.

Compared to our experience of family or private life, our social or public roles tend to be fairly clear-cut. If you're a secretary, truck driver, teacher, CEO, or at-home-parent, you've more than likely got a clear idea of what's expected of you. But the roles we play as son, daughter, sister, brother, father, mother, lover, friend, or spouse always take us into murkier emotional territory. We are much more blindly bound to yearnings, fears, hopes, terrors, and frustrations in our private lives. We are affected by family in ways we can't begin to fathom because for so long "family" was the only world we knew.

To an infant, Daddy and Mommy are Adam and Eve: language, food, comfort, morality, lessons about gender, learned behaviors of every kind all proceed from your first caregivers. We're not usually aware of their enormous power and how they affect our assumptions. We tend to be stuck in powerful dramas we can't begin to understand until we can find ways to take a larger and less-charged look at them. Only then can we tease out the nature of the "play" we've all tacitly agreed to perform and change the roles we're playing.

Acting Out and Shutting Down

Most people, when they feel afraid or overwhelmed by shock or conflict, experience a "word deficit." It's common at these times to revert to the feelings and sometimes the tactics of a two-year-old: either exploding into a tantrum or breaking down into inconsolable tearful despair. Emotions are too out-sized to handle with much reflection or thought: they urgently require expression—the quicker the better. This is why at times of great distress we tend to act before we think: the pain is too great to talk over "reasonably." But *how* each of us chooses to express our intolerable emotions directly—*why* we choose the particular means of expression we do at these times of extremity—are different for each of us and deserve close attention.

The first thing to remember is that you *are* making a choice—even if, in the explosive moment, it may seem like it's choosing you. What we're usually not aware of is that we'd been schooled to make these choices long ago, usually so long ago that by now they've become reflex. And often what that reflex tells us to do is shut down: we may "act" by refusing to communicate at all.

Krista and Anthony, a recently married young couple who came to me for counseling as the result of Krista's exasperation with Anthony's mother, offer a telling example. Krista complained to me in a couple-counseling session with Anthony: "From the moment we married, Anthony's mother has attacked me—for my housekeeping, for not giving Anthony the right food, for paying too much attention to my job, spending too much money—the list goes on. At first I just put up with it, but now it's gotten to the point where I've decided I just won't speak to her any more. That's it—I've had enough. I won't even take a phone call from the woman. Anthony may have to put up with her, but I'm not used to this kind of abuse, and I'm just not going to take it."

Anthony was miserable about the standoff. He knew there was a good deal of truth in what Krista was saying, but he was between a long-familiar rock and hard place. "Look," he said. "She's my mother. I've always had to deal with her criticism, put up with this. I know it's hard, but it's just how she is. I don't know why Krista can't learn to tough this out and not let it bother her so much. I mean, when you get married, you get the whole family package. If I could change my mother, I would. But I can't."

However, Krista wasn't the only one refusing to communicate with Anthony's mother. He didn't realize that he'd refused to communicate with his mother as well. Because he was so afraid to provoke her, his only mode was to placate her. It wasn't until Anthony began to realize that his mother's expectations were part of a family drama in which *he* had also taken part— that his subservience to his mother meant he had as much complicity in keeping this drama of abuse going as his mother did—that he began to be able to step out of that drama and heal from its toxic effects. Doing this not only ultimately enabled him to relate to his mother more openly—to stop shutting down and start communicating honestly with her—but helped him to communicate better with Krista as well.

How did he come to realize that he too was playing a role—and learn the benefits of changing it? It took the hard work of facing his fear that he might risk losing his mother's love by standing up to her. It also took restraint: learning that it wouldn't be profitable to spew out his backed-up anger—to abruptly change from placating his mother to berating her for a role she didn't know (and maybe would never know) she was playing. His task was simply— at first—to see and then decide not to play the kowtowing role in which his family drama had cast him.

The effects of our family dramas and the roles we're used to playing in them are profound. Anthony is coming to realize that his subservience to his mother has created a pattern in his life of subservience to many other people—especially anyone in authority. It's amazing how often we reenact old family patterns in the rest of our lives. Think of your own relationships, and ask yourself who in your family may be the model for the people who attract and repel you, or who you feel "make" you act in a certain way. It's not always so obvious that to some degree we've married or are working alongside Dad or Mom, but after you recognize that you may be playing a role that provokes other people to act like "mom" or "dad," the pattern—and your part in it—begins to reveal itself.

We resist seeing our own roles in a family drama partly because they're so familiar we don't know we can behave any other way. But there's an urgency about sticking to our roles, too—an urgency with two parts. On some level we feel that if we "trespass" or fail to act like we're "supposed" to, we'll be in danger; we'll lose our parents' love, we'll fail. We also keep playing our roles in the hope we'll "get it right this time." Anthony slowly woke up to this in his relationship with his mother: "I guess I always felt that if I could just be nice enough to my mother, she would lighten up. And since she never lightened up, I always assumed I was never being nice enough."

This brings us to what Freud called "repetition compulsion," the compulsion to repeat behaviors and reenact family dramas in the unconscious hope that we'll resolve the dilemmas that gave rise to the need to repeat them. The trap is, when you're in the grip of a repetition compulsion, you only know you're doing "what feels right." But, as Krista and Anthony have begun to see, "what feels right" sometimes turns out to be very wrong.

The Injustice Collector

Anthony's breakthrough came as he learned to understand that his mother was an injustice collector and he was a people pleaser. Every player in a family rift drama tends to enact one or the other of these roles. And if you don't become aware of your own role, you tend to play it for years—sometimes for a lifetime. Another client of mine, Barbara, offers a sad example: her own father. Her description of him gives us a good overall view of the traits of the typical injustice collector:

"My father always had a list of people who he felt had insulted, injured, or treated him unjustly. I thought of it as my dad's shit list. And I was often on that list. At one point, for various infractions most of which I had no idea I'd committed, he refused to talk to me for over five years. As he got older, his list grew and he became even more isolated, angry, and bitter. My mother was no help. Although she was a strong woman in every other aspect of her life— she was a well-respected junior high school principal—with my father she was a sniveling wimp, afraid to disagree with him for fear of one of his rages. Whenever my father exploded at me, she'd beg me to apologize to him. I did it to appease her, but I tell you, it was an awful house to grow up in."

It didn't take much to set Barbara's father off. "Like the time years ago they visited my mother's sister and were put up for the night in a guest room with an uncomfortable sleeper sofa next to a radiator that banged all night long. Okay, it was uncomfortable. But for my father, that ended the relationship for good. And it became a story he told for years afterward to anyone who'd listen. Till the day he died."

Barbara's father was later diagnosed with cancer, but becoming ill did nothing to soften him. "By that time he'd not only alienated everyone in his original family, his brothers and sisters—except for my mother, my sister Edna and me (and I was barely hanging on)—but everyone he'd ever known. He literally had no friends. When he was diagnosed with cancer, rather than trying to rally his family around him for support, he just got more abusive—his diatribes got worse. It was very sad to watch. He died when I was in my fifties. The only people at his funeral were my mother, sister, and me. And I think the only reason I attended was that I felt so bad for my mother. Even the few friends he'd made when my parents first moved to a retirement community in Arizona had deserted him—he'd picked fights with them, too, in his final months."

Unfortunately the roles Barbara and Edna's parents played bestowed them with an unwelcome legacy. Barbara tended to be a people pleaser like her mother was to her father; Edna has become a version of her harsh and critical injustice collector father. "This was almost more horrible than seeing my father do it—to see my sister acting as he did, ruining everyone's happiness.

Manipulating a story and presenting it in a way that would portray her family and herself as the poor pitiful victims of whoever in the family happened to be having a good day. For years, I just repeated my old pattern with her—apologizing and scrambling to make everything all right again."

Recently Barbara's son Lawrence got married, and he wanted his Aunt Edna and her husband to come to the wedding but, because it was a small wedding and there just wasn't room for them, he regretfully told his aunt that they wouldn't be able to accommodate her own married son and daughter and their kids. Predictably, Edna blew up and phoned Barbara in a rage. But Barbara had come to realize that Edna wasn't the only one who'd had enough. She was unwilling to keep playing the same role with her sister that she'd played with her father. Simply, without rancor, she replied to her sister: "Okay, goodbye."

Barbara sighs as she remembers that phone call—the last she's had with her sister for many months. "I don't know what if anything may bring us together again," Barbara says. "I only know that I saw my father ruin the lives of everyone around him and die bitter and alienated. I realized Edna seemed to be determined to play out that ugly drama, too. And I finally decided I didn't need or want to be a part of that."

If you're reading this book, the great likelihood is that you're a people pleaser worrying about pleasing an injustice collector. Look at the typical traits of the injustice collector. See who comes to mind.

Characteristics of Injustice Collectors

1. Injustice collectors are never wrong. How is it possible that they are never wrong? It's simple: They are always right.
2. Injustice collectors never apologize. Ever. For anything.
3. Injustice collectors truly believe they are morally and ethically superior to others and that others seem incapable of holding themselves to the same high standards as the injustice collector does.
4. Injustice collectors make the rules, break the rules, and enforce the rules of the family. They are a combination of legislator, police, judge, and jury to those they consider their subjects. They forever banish from their kingdom any subject they deem disloyal, and only grant clemency if there is sufficient contrition.
5. Injustice collectors never worry about what is wrong with them as their "bad list" grows. Their focus is always on the failings of others.

6. Injustice collectors are never troubled by the disparity between their rules for others and their own expectations of themselves.
7. Injustice collectors rationalize their own behavior with great ease and comfort.
8. Injustice collectors have an external orientation; the problem always exists in the world, outside of themselves, and in their view, the world would be an acceptable place if their rules and standards were followed at all times.
9. Injustice collectors do not have a capacity for remorse or guilt.
10. Injustice collectors scoff at the idea of therapy, therapists, self-help books, and other tools used by people who struggle to live with them.
11. The phrase *walking on eggshells* describes life with an injustice collector.

Tamara, a client of mine, told me that she had received a call from her sister Tina about a conflict Tina was having with their mother. Tamara was wary of getting involved—Tina was volatile, tended to rage out-of-control when she was crossed, and could be horribly abusive—ironically very like the mother whose abuse she was complaining about. Tamara and their brother Dennis played far more acquiescent roles. They'd all grown up with their angry mother's abuse, but Tamara and Dennis's people-pleasing tactics had kept them more out of their mother's line of fire.

Tina had recently started therapy, which gave her space to vent full-force about the mother who'd cursed and abused her throughout her life. She now turned to Tamara in the hope that she'd support her in ganging up to tell off their mom. When Tamara refused to get involved, Tina blew her top. (An injustice collector blowing his or her top is not a pretty sight.) Tina called her up and started yelling at her and telling Tamara that she had no clue as to how to act like a family member, and that she was tired of being treated with contempt and ridicule by her and their brother.

When Tamara tried to respond to Tina, she found herself being outshouted with accusations of betrayal, callousness, wimpiness, coldness, and stinginess. Tina's tone only got louder and louder as Tamara stammered and tried to get a word in edgewise. Tina finally told her that she was a laughingstock and "fatter than a pig." Tamara simply replied, "Stop it or I'll hang up on you,

Tina," to which Tina responded with a loud "Drop dead" as she slammed down the phone.

I've subjected you to excerpts of Tina's rage at Tamara not to invite you to gang up on Tina—and certainly not to make fun of her rage. I submit it as a reminder of the terrible things that get said in the heat of a family breakup. The words aren't pretty. Whatever is at hand gets thrown—no holds barred. When injustice collectors are determined to hurt someone, there seems no end to the weapons and poison they can wield to cause harm.

We'll see later on in this chapter how Tamara managed to deal with Tina, but now let's first look at the characteristics of the people-pleaser—the yin to the yang of the injustice collector.

The People Pleaser

We've already met a number of people pleasers. Barbara, Anthony, and Tamara have all enacted the role of people pleaser in relation to the injustice collectors who were making their lives hell. We don't have to go into much further detail: having discussed people who've attempted to assuage and placate injustice collectors, we've already painted a fairly detailed picture of this role. So let's just recap briefly—with this brief addition—which is that, sadly, for all their attempts to please, few people pleasers tend to be really pleased with anything themselves. People pleasers are generally full of self-doubt, self-blame, shame, and humiliation. They go to great lengths to get love and approval from others, but no matter how much they get, they rarely feel loved or good about themselves.

Here's a good depiction of the people pleaser, as conveyed to me by one client who had always seen himself playing the role:

"I felt like it was my fault when it rained, and that if I was stronger, better, smarter, or nicer, that the rain wouldn't fall. When my dad had a bad day at work and came home all tanked up on Jack Daniels, I felt responsible for his anger and unhappiness and thought that I should do something about it quickly. When my mom was frustrated at her inability to pull together a career for herself, I thought it was my fault, and that if I only would do something differently, that my Mom would be okay."

Does this—or anything in the following list—sound familiar?

Characteristics of a People Pleaser

1. People pleasers are reactive to events, situations, and interactions, rarely taking the initiative to assert their own needs, wants, and desires into a situation.
2. People pleasers take any criticism as fact, and immediately suffer a deflation in their own self-esteem.
3. People pleasers feel an extraordinary fear of abandonment.
4. People pleasers blame themselves for everything that ever goes wrong.
5. People pleasers become more concerned with others' feelings than their own.
6. People pleasers have an overdeveloped sense of responsibility, expecting of themselves magical abilities to fix the significant others in their lives.
7. People pleasers learned early in their lives to bury their own feelings, needs, and wants, and keep them buried until they get help for their problems.
8. People pleasers chronically confuse pity with love and self-sacrifice with caring for others.

The Courage to Change Your Role

When Tamara worked with me in therapy, she began to understand much more about the ways she'd always been a people pleaser—having grown up with two injustice collectors, her mother and her sister Tina. She was quite traumatized by the letter she received from Tina, and decided, for once in her life, not to respond, and to let the issue die. "I've been begging her for forgiveness for things I didn't do my whole life. My entire childhood was spent hiding from her and my mother. My mother's become manageable. Tina hasn't. I can't play this role anymore. If she says she wants out of our family, it's fine with me."

Some months later, Tamara became engaged to her boyfriend. Shortly after that, her brother Dennis told her he had reconciled with Tina, and that Tina now wanted to reconcile with her. When Tina called her, Tamara was very reluctant to talk to her for fear of being hurt again, but Tina congratulated her so warmly about her engagement and seemed so excited about her marriage, Tamara decided—hopefully—that maybe Tina had turned over a new leaf. However, when it came time to plan the wedding, Tamara found herself in a terrible bind with her family once again.

It was clear to me that the drama Tamara had been in all her life was starting again. I suggested she once again felt paralyzed—stuck between her mother and sister—terrified that they would ruin her wedding. They still weren't talking to each other, both wanted to be at Tamara's wedding, and Tamara feared, quite reasonably, that her wedding would become a fiasco of a confrontation if they both were invited to attend.

I asked Tamara to pick out three words that she felt had characterized her role in her family drama throughout her life. She came up with *weak*, *fragile*, and *wounded*. I said to her that that's how she was acting in the present, and she agreed. Then I asked her to come up with the three best antonyms to these words. She replied, "*Strong, tough,* and *able*."

"OK, then, Tamara, your task is clear. Rewrite the drama and make your character strong, tough, and able. That new character will know just what to do."

What Tamara was able to do here is key. She could begin—with a few simple descriptive words—to see how she might actually be able to change the role of people pleaser she'd played throughout her life. "Strong, tough, and able" are words she repeats to herself when she feels as if she might sink back down to people-pleasing acquiescence. They fill her with a new sense of who she might be—who she can choose to be. She can trust this sense to guide her about how to act—not *react* in the old, fearful ways.

Diane is a woman who offers another telling example of learning to change a lifelong role. Her mother died tragically of breast cancer in 1967 at age thirty-eight. After her mother's death Diane married. She also ultimately raised her two younger sisters because their father's alcoholism had made him incapable of doing that. After decades of drama and conflict, Diane's father married his third wife and disowned his daughters, writing them out of his will. Right at about this time Diane was diagnosed with breast cancer. Thankfully she seems to have beaten it, but she tells me it really opened her eyes to how she had been living.

"I survived cancer and I survived an alcoholic father and I survived losing my mother when I was nineteen and bringing up my younger sisters. I'm done with trying to please unreasonable people. When my father disowned us, my sisters and I were devastated, and it took me years to realize it was his loss. I spent the first fifty years of my life playing out the role of a weak, undeserving, whipping girl, and since my cancer, I've come to realize . . . and act . . . deserving, strong, and unwilling to take anyone's abuse." Deserving, strong, unwilling to take abuse. These are now Diane's watchwords. The need for them has arisen out of painful experience; they aren't verbal band-aids she tries to believe are true. They are true.

Arrested Development

As we grow and develop through our lifetimes, we all attempt to learn how best to meet our needs and to find the best ways of helping the people we love to meet theirs. In childhood, our needs are mostly tended to. As we mature, we learn to operate beyond what psychologists call "need-gratifying levels" to more interdependent and mutually nurturing ways of relating to other people. All of us feel like we're operating at optimum capacity when our interpersonal relationships are based on mutual respect and generosity. However, we all also have times when our own needs become paramount—when we want what *we* want—and we operate at less mature and more dependent levels of functioning.

In a family that functions well, only children operate in a need-gratifying manner. The adults have moved on to more mature ways of relating interpersonally. In the family that severs ties with family members, however, this kind of maturity is rarely achieved. The injustice collector acts as an overgrown infant, only concerned about meeting his or her own needs for gratification. The people pleaser is locked into the vain attempt to accommodate the injustice collector. Unable to move beyond insults and slights, whether real or imagined, injustice collectors become consumed with three basic issues:

1. What they feel people did *to them* that was unnecessarily mean, hurtful, and thoughtless
2. What people did *not* do for them that they feel they should have done
3. When they feel the people in their lives have *not* done *enough* for them

As with small children, it never occurs to them, ever, that not everything is about them. In this way, they operate on the level of infants who believe themselves to be the center of the world.

Healing the Wounds of Self-Esteem That Trap You in a Role

not one or the other

The people pleaser and the injustice collector suffer the same deficits of self-esteem. Basically, injustice collectors suffer from the belief that they can never get enough—and yet *deserve* to get—unending attention, admiration, and adoration, as well as blind obedience to their dictates. Without this, self-esteem plummets. People pleasers, paradoxically, have the same problem in regulating self-esteem, although they deal with it differently. While injustice collectors are overprotective of their damaged selves, people pleasers are under-protective, and disregard their own needs to preserve their integrity.

In the context of my family of origin, until not too long ago I had always been a people pleaser. Every time my father or my sister felt that my wife or I had done something unnecessarily mean, hurtful, or thoughtless to them, I apologized, was contrite, asked for forgiveness, and took the rap fully and without question. At the same time, I learned to absorb and accept the very same kind of slights that were perpetrated on me, putting up with behavior and treatment that neither my father nor sister would have ever tolerated. I felt, understandably, as battered, bruised, and hurt as they did, but I chose the apologetic, people-pleasing route to be loved rather than the demanding, angry route. When I finally decided that the way I was playing out my family drama was too damaging to my own integrity, autonomy, and well-being, I was able to pull out of the role I had played my whole life.

I also realized that in my family drama a very limited number of character traits were available to the players. In my mind, either I could be weak, wimpy, submissive, and pathetic, or I could be a raging tyrant and bully who demanded total compliance from everyone in my realm. The notions of being strong and assertive while staying calm, insisting on appropriate boundaries and on being treated with respect and dignity, were not in my realm of experience. Once I realized that I was much happier with the person I was in the rest of my life, I realized it was foolish not to be that "me" around my family as well. I began to feel liberated and genuinely felt they could take the new me or leave it. So far, they've chosen to leave it, but I feel a sense of integrity and self-respect that I had never experienced before.

Family Life Is like Any Other Group

In fundamental ways, families operate very much as any other group does—from psychotherapy to business to a large group such as a nation. Every group must find ways to work out conflicts to achieve tasks. The task of the family is to meet its family members' needs. The task of a business is to make money. The task of a nation is to govern and maintain order. When a group works, its tasks are accomplished.

However, when a group does not work, it becomes a fight-flight group. In a business that has reached the fight-flight stage, there is dissension, disharmony, and a lack of productivity—and the business will go under if some means aren't found to make it work again. When a nation is not functioning, either a civil war will ensue or war will be declared to deflect the dissatisfaction of citizens onto some outside scapegoat or cause. When a family cannot resolve its conflicts and cannot meet the needs of its members, the fight-flight proposition also comes into play. Something must be done, or—like a business or nation—the family group will fall apart.

The fight-flight family model is clearly evident in Tamara's family. Tina's insistent demands for attention, validation, and recognition, and her attempts to meet those demands by bullying and intimidation, as well as a dysfunctional plea for unity and solidarity against the mother, all spell disaster—not just for Tina, but for the family as a whole. Tamara has always attempted to get the same needs for attention, validation, and recognition met through pleasing and placating, but these are as doomed as Tina's bullying tactics: they never work because the peace they may momentarily lead to never lasts. Tina is fighting—Tamara is fleeing the fight—and the family cannot survive. For the moment, all Tamara can do is realize she has the power to stop the tug-of-war—which she has done.

Sometimes this is all you can do. Sadly, not all family rifts can be mended or resolved. But when there is hope of reunion, each member must feel sufficient autonomy—and healthy self-esteem—for a reunion to last. Insight can start to bolster that self-esteem—the insight, once again, of realizing you don't have to play the same fight-or-flight role you've been playing.

For example, when injustice collectors gain insight about the futility of their mode, they can learn to find new ways of meeting their needs. A client of mine, Joyce, has come to realize she is an injustice collector when it comes to her mother-in-law. Like Krista who can't get along with her husband Anthony's mother, Joyce freely acknowledges to me that she and her mother-in-law don't like each other, and she's often felt attacked and hurt by her. "I'd like her out of my life and our life altogether, but I just can't do that to my husband. He acknowledges she's difficult, but she's his mother after all.

"I realized when I'm around her, I feel like I'm in a war zone. I'm just waiting for the next attack and insult to come my way. I find myself either wanting to get away or to fight with her. But the thing is, she's *not* always attacking and she's not always so awful, and in many ways, even if she's not particularly loving to me, she's good to my husband and our kids. It's just I find myself being terrified of being blindsided by one of her nasty critical jabs, caught unprepared. So I'm always ready for combat, but I guess that being aware of it helps me to control it.

"I saw my parents fighting all the time about my grandmother—my mother couldn't stand her mother-in-law either—and I experienced the pain of the cutoffs my mother and grandmother created intermittently throughout my life. I'm motivated to remain cognizant of this, and despite the fact I'm sure Colin's mother and I will never be great friends, I'm pleased that I find I can control myself and not create the misery for my husband and children that my mother and grandmother created for my dad and me and my brother."

Jacob Moreno was the founder of a therapeutic technique called psychodrama in which he asked patients to act out dramatic scenarios from his or her own life. His wife, Zerka Moreno, explained his techniques in the following way: "Act yourself as you never were. . . . Be your own . . . playwright, your own actor, your own therapist, and finally, your own creator." We just saw how Joyce did this, and ultimately, this is the choice we all also face with our families. Of course, not everyone—and certainly not every injustice collector—has the insight Joyce has, and not everyone is willing to put in the effort to be their own playwright. As we go on, we'll find more varied ways to do so.

But remember: we didn't learn our modes of acting out—our roles—yesterday. Indeed, as you've seen in the brief recap I've given of my own life, the tensions and tugs-of-war that ultimately resulted in my parents' rejection of me had, in fact, lifelong roots. It's helpful at this vulnerable stage of acceptance to realize that this acting out more than likely has been going on throughout your whole life. This is the time, gently, to begin to tally up those instances of acting out that have characterized not only your family's treatment of you and each other, but of your own complicity in the drama. And family dramas thrive on complicity. As you begin to see each family member's mode of acting out, you begin to see what their roles have been throughout the years—the archetypal functions each of you has unwittingly agreed to perform or been pressured into performing.

Characterizing family roles in our own language can be very clarifying—giving us clues about our own modes of acting out as well as our family members' roles. Seeing myself as the groveling peacemaker is an example. Not only did it tell me how I tended to act out, but it suggested how I might want consciously to change my behavior.

Again, this stage involves observation more than interpretation. Just see who your family members are in terms of the roles they play in your family. As you begin to see how they act out—and how you do—you'll eventually also see what all of you are afraid of being and doing. This will enable you to effect some helpful changes later on, if not in your family members' actions, then in your own.

4

Understand Your Family Myths

The last conversation I had with my father, in January 2001, was about the fact that I had not called my sister in a timely manner to congratulate her on the engagement of her son. The conversation deteriorated from there, culminating in his telling me I would never again be welcome in his home. The tardiness of my congratulatory phone call was the excuse for the estrangement.

However, the unspoken reasons were of course the more important ones—as they are in every family estrangement. It is the unspoken reasons that we need to understand, because they help us discover the Family Myths that provoke us into playing the roles we defined in the last chapter. Becoming aware of those myths help us begin to live our lives with an unprecedented freedom. Family Myths are strangling. Getting out of their grip is crucial to healing—not only from the effects of a family rift, but from many wounds that affect us in every realm of life.

Family Myths are cherished by the people who—however unwittingly—have brought them into being. In my own situation, what my father was really saying to me during that unfortunate phone call was that I had shattered our family's myth: the myth of a close and tight-knit family in which everyone was in complete agreement about everything, that is, in complete agreement with my father. I had violated one of the tenets of this myth in a way that was unforgivable to him. For that, my punishment was to be expelled from the family.

Lori, whom we met a couple chapters back, had also shattered her family's myth by becoming independent and saying no to being battered and abused by her husband. Her mother and sister allegedly took her son away because they feared she was becoming a drug addict. That was the excuse for their acting in a way that made it impossible for Lori to feel she could ever have a close and loving relationship with them. But the unspoken reason had to do with her emerging autonomy and independence, intolerable to a family who valued only submission.

Jason too dispelled a Family Myth: that of a perfectly normal family—even though one brother had a drug problem and another was severely depressed. They *looked* normal on the outside, and Jason's parents could reassure themselves with that fact. Jason partnering with a man, however, dispelled that myth far too blatantly to be tolerated—so intolerably that it provoked the rage of his parents and eventually resulted in the estrangement that caused him and them so much pain and anguish. Jason's transgression meant that they had to acknowledge that the perfect family they imagined they had was simply a fantasy.

Fortunately, both Lori and Jason were strong enough to realize that the family could survive the destruction of the myth. Indeed, Jason eventually felt stronger once he was able to come out of the closet and be himself. His brothers too are likely to recover from their problems if they get the proper help and receive their parents' support in doing so. The signs for Jason's family are good. They are, of course, not so good in many other cases. Family Myths die hard.

The Sources of Family Myth

What is the Family Myth and why does it have so much power over our individual growth and our family relations? What happens when the Family Myth, nurtured and prized for so long, meets its match at the hands of inevitable change? The answers to these questions can be shattering.

The Family Myth comprises various well-rehearsed notions, wholly false, about the nature of the family unit. The Family Myth dictates that surface appearance is more important than individual happiness: that what "ought to" be true must squelch what is true. The Family Myth involves the presumption that every family member is compatible, possesses the same goals, and loves all the others without question. The Family Myth is a fantasy predicated on a like-it-or-not unified "we."

Common Family Myths generally are framed as "we" statements. "We all get along wonderfully." "We all have the same goals and like the same people." "We are all loving and accepting people, and we believe in democracy and choice." The Family Myth does not usually allow for "I" statements. The Family Myth does not readily tolerate individual choice, different points of view, or difference of opinion.

David, whom we met in Chapter 1—whose grown son Craig refused to speak with him, his wife Marie, or their son, Craig's eight-year-old half-brother—had to dispel the myths about his blended family in a way that was quite painful to him. He had to acknowledge that not only did it seem that Craig did not like Marie, him, or their son—neither did David like Craig when Craig acted like this. They were not a family who got along well at all. In fact, they seemed to greatly dislike each other. "It's awful to acknowledge this," said David, "but I guess dealing with reality puts me ahead of the game if I ever get the opportunity to sit down in the same room again with Craig."

The Power of Family Myth over Growth

Why does the Family Myth have so much power over our individual growth and our family relations?

Family Myths are generally fantasies about the love, support, and caring nature of one's family of origin. This is what makes the dissolution of the Family Myth so terribly profound and earth shattering. Following are some typical Family Myth statements: "We are a close-knit family. We love to spend holidays together. We tend to agree on the important issues, and when we can't agree, we compromise readily. We all stick together in times of trouble, and support each other when necessary."

It's basically an idealized fiction of what ought to be, because, in fact, most well-functioning families do have some level of disharmony, dissent, discussion, sweat, and tears along with some consensus and moments of harmony. Conflict is normal and healthy in a family that works well: it tends to be seen as abnormal in one that does not. It is very easy to be caught up in the fiction of a Family Myth. The families we envision when our own Family Myths are born are always composed of happier, cleaner, better people than we are or can be. Of course a further glitch is that we don't always *actually* want to be what it is that we *think* we want to be. The resulting conflict between what we want in theory and what we want in reality is often a destructive one.

In most cases, the fashioning of the Family Myth is not a democratic process. Not everyone even gets a say as to what the Family Myth is going to be. Despite the decidedly undemocratic way in which the Family Myth is initially established, the idea of being shinier, better versions of ourselves or having the unconditional love and support of every family member is a seductive one. Con-sequently, in families where the Family Myth is actively propagated, we all eventually buy in. The pervasive and persuasive nature of the Family Myth is the reason you don't see blue Mohawk hairstyles in Norman Rockwell paintings.

When David continued to talk about what went on in his family and his relationship with his son Craig, he acknowledged that the years when he and Craig's mother were having marital problems were difficult ones for Craig. Holidays were awful, and generally fraught with family feuds. When he and Craig's mother separated, Craig wasn't happy, and David wasn't the greatest at being supportive. When David started dating Marie, he didn't have an easy time listening to Craig's negative feelings about their relationship.

"I admit I wasn't father of the year, but I also have to tell you Craig wasn't a piece of cake, and his mother, my ex-wife, wasn't any walk in the park either. We all did the best we could, and I wish Craig could realize that. I just don't think total excommunication is merited, although now that I acknowledge the myths that I lived with, and expected Craig to live with, I can understand how he could feel the way he feels."

When a family member chooses and performs an act of independence—like a blue Mohawk, or marrying someone of another race, or devotion to an unusual hobby, or embarking on a career other than the family business—the Family Myth is often threatened, and a rupture between family members almost inevitably results. The typical response to such a threat, by a family under the sway of the Family Myth, is swift retribution or even a family "divorce," whereby the offending family member is cast out.

The Effects of Change

What happens when the Family Myth, nurtured and prized (at least by its creators) for so long, encounters the inevitable change?

In some cases people we see who are going through a shattering family "divorce" persist in following the laws of the Family Myth to a T, not realizing that the myth is not necessarily what will actually make themselves or their family happy. In other cases, individuals in the family make choices or decisions that are blatantly in opposition to the Family Myth, causing deep rifts between family members.

Recall how Deborah turned to Al-Anon for support when her dad would not support her marriage to Jacques, her African-American fiancé. She also shattered a myth in her family, one of normalcy, and broke the denial of her dad's alcoholism. Deborah's uncovering of the myth in her family allowed her the opportunity to rewrite her life story with a whole new perspective, and to begin her married life with entirely different choices, values, and opportunities than she would otherwise have had.

Grace had always been Daddy's girl and Mom's mommy. After her parents' divorce, Grace accompanied her dad to social events and was his best pal. Her mom, on the other hand, wallowed in depression and drug abuse for years after the divorce. Grace cleaned the house, cooked, and tried to be her mom's therapist and best friend. Grace came to therapy to work on developing her career as a singer and actress in musical theater. She also worked out her poor choices of men, and ended up marrying Rod, a successful restaurateur. Not surprisingly, along the way she also became an independent adult, and stopped the dysfunctional behavior that kept her tied to her parents.

Grace stopped being the caregiver for her mom, and instead gave her the name of a therapist. She began to relate to her dad in more age-appropriate daughterly ways rather than as companion and spouse substitute. Then, after she announced her engagement to Rod, both her parents stopped speaking to her. Grace was shattered. She was shocked to realize that neither of her parents wanted to have connections and lives of their own, and that they resented and envied Grace's new life. In this instance, the Family Myth was a rather dingy and broken-down one—not the utopian familial vision to which most families subscribe. However, in the most dysfunctional of families, it is not at all uncommon for the Family Myth to be the picture of dysfunction: "If I'm messed up, then you'd better be, too."

Family members pay a high price for going against the grain. Grace had tired of putting her own life on hold and forced her parents to release her. Deborah made the choice to defy her dad and walk away from his abusive tirades and reaped the benefits of self-respect and autonomy. Powerless in the face of these decisions, family members responded with "divorce," the casting out of the offending family member.

Births, deaths, marriages, aging, holidays, retirement, career successes, business failures—all the ups and downs of life—all have the potential for challenging the Family Myth and creating shattering scenarios for individuals. Both Grace and Deborah were devastated by their family's rejection of them. The loss of their parents' approval shook the very foundation of their lives, leaving them hurt, disoriented, and depressed.

When Life's Transitions Become Overwhelming: Denial

When a lifestyle change constitutes crisis or catastrophe too overwhelming to process and integrate, we often resort to that most primitive of defense mechanisms: denial. Whether it's a diagnosis of terminal illness, an IRS audit, a child being diagnosed with a serious health problem, or complete rejection by one's family of origin, the first response is generally one of a temporary psychological blindness, which slowly clears as the scope and intensity of the particular tragedy can be integrated.

While denial may seem foolish immediately to those on the outside or later to those involved, it's completely normal as a first response to a trauma. Such a trauma can be so overwhelming that we resort to "magical thinking" that may be just what we need at that moment to buffer ourselves from the shock. We often try to believe that the problem will somehow magically fix itself. Being cut off by a family member feels like being killed off. We tend to react to this cutoff with many of the same emotions we bring to any process of mourning. And now it often feels as if we're mourning our own deaths as much as the death of whoever has cut us off—a process made more painful because we rarely receive support for it (no one, technically, has died). This is very confusing. And sometimes all we want to do is to pull the shades down over everything and pretend it's not happening.

Again, in the short term, to lessen the initial force of the pain we feel, this may not be so bad. But when it continues, it is a problem.

Amanda was in denial for most of her adult life about the myth that had been perpetrated by her extended family of origin. "When I was a child, my father, mother, and I were part of an extended family that included my father's parents and three sisters and their families. My mother's parents weren't alive, but her sister lived close by. When I was nine years old, my forty-three-year-old father died of a brain tumor. On the night he died, his parents, sister, and brother-in-law walked out of the hospital, leaving my mother to make the necessary arrangements and get home by herself.

"That was the end of my life in my father's family. Shortly thereafter, my father's parents sued my mother, claiming that my father owed them money. They didn't show up in court, and the case was dropped, but it did add to my mother's grief and anguish. She got remarried to Sal a few years later, when I was eleven. All of a sudden I was thrust into my stepfather's home with his two kids. He was a drunk, and I saw a side of my mother that must have lain dormant her whole life. She started drinking with Sal and then the two of them would get into horrible fights. The neighbors would call the police— they sounded that bad. Between my mother's screaming hysterics and my stepfather's drunken tirades of abuse, my stepsiblings and I would all be freaked out and hysterical ourselves.

"By the time I was twelve I began to stand up to my parents, which was something that didn't go over real big with Sal. The more out of control they got, the more out of control I would get. Sal kept threatening me that he was going to 'send me away,' and one day, out of the blue, the two of them took me to a hospital where they talked the doctors into admitting me to the psych ward for depression.

"My entire world had really collapsed now, and soon I was placed in a residential treatment facility, which is a polite way of saying orphanage. I did okay with that, and it was sure better than being with my mother and Sal. The problem began after my children were born. Thank God, by this time my mother had left Sal and sobered up. I had already established myself in my career, and now that I had a family of my own felt very proud of myself. That was when my mother began criticizing me for working while my children were small.

"That was not so problematic, but when I told her she had to stop, she said, 'Look. I raised you and I stayed home. Look at how you've turned out.' It was as if someone took a paper bag off of my head, because I blurted out, 'That's not true. You didn't raise me. I was raised in an orphanage.' With that, Mom stormed off in a rage, telling me I was ungrateful, unappreciative, and a liar. I, of course, was so shaken by all of it that I returned her shouts with accusations of my own.

"I don't know how I walked around in such denial for so long, but it occurred to me that despite having been able to sustain a relationship with my mother, and even with all the hard work I had done in therapy to come to terms with my life, I had never before really acknowledged that *I had raised myself.* My husband's family was actually under the impression that she had raised me, as were the few friends she had made in recent years.

"Something in me made me realize that this myth really diminished my experience. I mean, the orphanage really wasn't that bad in many regards. It was kind of like being at camp year-round, except that the staff, as loving as they could be at times, were being paid to be 'house parents,' and there was always a feeling of loneliness no matter how hard the staff there tried to create a festive feeling.

"When I didn't hear from my mother for two weeks after our blow-up, I began to get worried. I called and she wouldn't return my calls. I left messages, and when I finally reached her at home she asked me, 'Who is this?' 'It's Amanda,' I said. She answered, 'Oh. I don't know anyone named Amanda,' and then she hung up on me.

"I decided to go to her house. Surely she would talk to me if I showed up. She did, but with the chain lock on the apartment door, willing to talk but keeping me barred from her home. I told her I just didn't want to pretend anymore, that I loved her but needed her to acknowledge what it must have been like for me growing up. She said that I exaggerated and dramatized everything, and that I'd always been a big drama queen.

"That was four months ago and she still won't talk with me. Now I understand why I needed to use denial for so long. Now I feel strong enough to honestly look at my life, and, in reality, I was abandoned by my mother when I was thirteen. She rarely visited me at the residence, and I rarely visited because the house was full of vodka bottles and Sal's rage—evidenced by the unrepaired holes in the wall he had smashed. I was already finished with college by the time my mother left Sal and became sober. I'm grateful that she did, and I'm hoping that she'll get over her current rage with me. I needed to use denial for many years, and then suddenly it stopped working for me."

Appreciating Denial—and Moving Beyond It

The point here, as with every emotion in the wake of being exiled by the family, is to appreciate the temporary use of denial—and forgive yourself for employing it when you do. Just remember that denial can work against you—and be reassured by Amanda's example that you *can* survive looking uncomfortable facts more directly in the face. It's normal if you respond to this necessity first by shutting down on even deeper levels. There's no easy way to deal with being cut off by people you thought loved you—or to face the reasons they cut you off.

Amanda was in a particularly tough position because she was only thirteen when her mother and stepfather basically abandoned her. Amanda's current situation with her mother, she feels, pales by comparison to the difficulties she had to face earlier in her life, and she hopes her mother will come around and, for once, give her the acceptance and acknowledgment that she needs. She knows that if she gives that need up, as she has always done, that her mother would come back into her life. She hoped now that her mother could finally summon the strength to give up her mythic story about Amanda's life and acknowledge what really happened, as well as stop criticizing her for being a working mother. Amanda needed her mother to do this without Amanda having to negate her own needs for acknowledgment and acceptance.

Why do we hang onto our denial? Why are we so afraid to say what we really mean, think and feel? Fear—but fear of very particular kinds.

The Family Myth is both a distortion of history as well as a misperception of the unspoken rules for maintaining peace within the family and what it takes to make other family members happy. Generally, the themes of the myth in a family are related to maintaining a lack of choice and freedom for individuals within the family unit, as a way of keeping the family glued together. Use the checklist below to think about the myth in your family and how it's been disrupted and caused the estrangement that you're experiencing right now. See how you can rewrite your history when you're able to look honestly at the potential components of family myths in the following list:

Checklist for Identifying Family Myths
- I have the freedom to say how I truly feel.
- I will have my painful feelings of hurt, loneliness, and rejection responded to with empathy.

- My attempts to communicate with my family members will be welcomed.
- I will continue to be liked, no matter what I think or feel.
- If I assert myself, I will be listened to and responded to in an appropriate and nonrejecting manner.
- No one in the family will attempt to humiliate or shame me for my choices or thoughts.
- I can express myself on the most delicate of topics without fearing an irreparable mess.
- I will not be laughed at or criticized for my choices in life or my feelings.
- I will still be welcome in my family no matter how far away I move.
- My choice of life partner will be accepted by my family members.
- My occupational choices will be respected by my family members.

If you need clarification, think about how Amanda rewrote her history after she became a mother. She thought her own mother would welcome her self-expression and attempts at communication. She thought her decision to be a working mother would be valued and respected. She did not think she would encounter an irreparable mess by expressing herself. She felt that if she asserted herself, her mother would respond to her in an appropriate and non-rejecting manner. These were all components of Amanda's family myth that were shattered by her inevitable growth when she became a parent. The rest of this chapter will give you more help in uncovering the myths in your family, so feel free to continue rewriting your history as you understand more about the myths with which you've been living.

Why Are Some Families Able to Get Past Their Myths?

There are two basic modes of conflict resolution possible within families. Functional families are able to cooperate and diplomatically resolve conflict, so that compromises and mutual acceptance can be attained. Happily, many families can cope with challenging changes and transitions, and the above-mentioned fears do not turn out to be true. A client of mine recently came out of the closet as a gay man and feared his family's rejection because of this. He was happily surprised that the myth of normalcy that he felt his family subscribed to was just that, a myth of his own creation.

Another client feared being cut off by his Orthodox Jewish parents when he announced his intention to marry his Vietnamese girlfriend. He was delighted to see that his parents, while not happy, took a position that he was their son no matter how different his choices were from what they would have wanted for him. These are families that can cope with differences in choice and belief when members go through life-cycle transitions. These are families who offer each other unconditional love.

When Families Cannot Get Past Their Myths

Families that cut off, on the other hand, tend to vacillate between avoidance and explosiveness; they hide, avoid, and ignore difficulties and deny real conflict until World War III breaks out. Thus, the family that cuts off generally is bogged down by a dysfunctional Family Myth whose dissolution inevitably leads to estrangement. Love is conditional on compliance to the myth in these families.

As we have seen in earlier chapters, family estrangement can be provoked by any number of scenarios. A family cutoff is a breakdown in communication: a severing of diplomatic ties much as two nations break diplomatic relations. Talking, compromises, mutual accommodation all have broken down and thus there can be no shared experience, shared pleasure, or interaction of any kind.

What we perceive as psychological problems tends to be a mirror of the current culture and fluctuates over time. When Freud formulated his classical theories of psychoanalysis, people's central concern was how to live with their drives, most notably their sexual and aggressive instincts.

Since then, our culture has evolved and changed radically; acceptance of our inner drives is now more common and, in fact, very much more a part of the fabric of our society. A central problem that has emerged more recently is the phenomenon of character disorders, people whose development has been arrested at a stage of an immature and fragile sense of self. The person with what is called a self disorder is vulnerable to what they experience as assaults on their self-esteem and are subject to rapid plummeting of their sense of self-worth.

Suffice it to say that these are the characters that create family estrangement. Most of us are all too familiar with these types of people and know the extreme difficulty of trying to live with them. These are the characters we met in the last chapter whom we dubbed injustice collectors; they have been allowed to assume leadership roles in the families that cut off members for various reasons.

Generally, these persons' very negative feelings about themselves are masqueraded as grandiosity and haughtiness, so that it's easy to forget how badly they really feel about themselves. Most of us easily confuse their aggressiveness and imperiousness as signs of power and strength. Their difficulty managing their anger causes most of us to instinctively submit because of how frightening and unpleasant their rages feel to us. When people make life transitions, whether in terms of marital status, socio-economic status, geographic location, or family composition, the family member with a fragile sense of self can easily feel mortally wounded, and that is when estrangements are bound to occur. When an injustice collector feels threatened by a family member's different life-style choice or value system or fears that their family member is moving too far away, either figuratively or literally, they find themselves with a limited repertoire of action. That is when they are likely to say, "Get out of my life."

Life-Cycle Events Challenge Our Adaptive Capacities

Family estrangements are usually triggered by the challenges of growth and change that occur in all lives as people reach transition periods in their lives. These transitions—like birth, school, college, marriage, children, grandchildren, death—can lead either to personal growth or to some degree of disintegration. The outcome of each stage is not always immediately evident, but each crisis in a family and each eventual family estrangement can be traced back to a transition in the family life cycle and a seminal event in that family's evolution. A given transition may either bring about growth for family members, or it may result in a breakdown in communications and a deterio-

ration in functioning for a given family member. Ultimately, the challenge of mastering a life transition may be so enormous that it will create the dissolution of a family as a whole, as we find in a family estrangement.

Families who disown their members always have long histories of ambivalence and difficulty resolving their problems with each other. Ultimately the feelings that occur after an estrangement are the very feelings that have been festering for years and even for decades. While there may have been a loving relationship of sorts, it was a relationship predicated on conditional love, a love that precluded freedom of thought and choice.

Herein lies one of the paradoxes of family estrangements: they have decades of brewing and developing that seem to culminate, unpredictably, in a defining moment of the life-long relationship. There is always the feeling in each family that a single act or gesture "caused" the cutting off of the family member, but this is never the case. In each case it is the culmination of years or even decades of disharmony and dysfunction, and some kind of rebellion against the Family Myth. Yet within each triumphant grasping of independence or authenticity, there is some degree of shame and doubt about one's inability to negotiate a mutually satisfying manner of interacting with a loved one. Before the triumph of full autonomy can be celebrated, the shame needs to be worked out and mourned.

Autonomy Disrupts the Family Myth

Declaring one's autonomy is a surefire way to ignite the furies of the family member who greedily desires to have the psychological upper hand over all who claim to love him or her.

"I've always had to walk on eggshells with my sister Lisa," Alice told me. Ever since I can remember, if Lisa didn't get her way there'd be hell to pay. My father was like that too, and when we were kids I truly believed he knew best. He and Lisa clashed continually, and somehow when he died, Lisa moved into his role, and the myth she tried to perpetrate was 'Lisa knows best.' Disagreement within my family meant betrayal, and it still does as far as Lisa is concerned. Whenever I've disagreed with her, it's been taken as a slap in the face rather than a difference of opinion. I mean, she's always been fine if you yes her to death, even if you don't mean it.

"Recently Lisa had what I guess is called a nervous breakdown in the middle of September. She and her husband had divorced some years before, and her daughter had just left for college. I guess it was the stress of living alone for the first time in her life. She called me and told me that she had started therapy, and that she discovered that we were both children of alcoholics. Well, this was nothing new to me; I had talked about it in therapy years ago.

"She also told me that she thought I had to go to meetings of Adult Children of Alcoholics, and she became furious with me when I told her I thought I didn't need to go. Lisa's motto has always been, 'If you're not with me, you're against me.' I told her I was with her and completely supported her efforts to get herself together again, but at the same time I don't feel it's good for me to rehash our lousy childhood continually. It depresses and upsets me, and I get no comfort from it. When I told Lisa I couldn't talk about this anymore with her, she flew into a rage, called me names, and cursed at me.

"The following day I received a completely poisonous e-mail from her. She said the cruelest things imaginable, and I just felt so hurt and angry. She then said she never wanted to see me or speak to me again, as if this behavior made me want to be closer to her. I realized it's been crap like this for almost forty years now between us, and I really feel it's so negative I can't do it anymore. I know she wants me to apologize and tell her I was wrong and she was right, but I just can't do that now. I didn't do anything wrong, and I didn't do anything to hurt her at all.

"The part that's most upsetting to me now is how awful I feel having no living family at all, at least no nuclear family. I have my aunt and uncle, and they haven't spoken to Lisa in years after she had a similar episode with them. It's just that it feels lonely and awful to have no relatives really that I can count on."

It's interesting here to see how Lisa had reconstructed a kind of second-stage Family Myth without realizing it—one in which "You're either with me or against me" was still the operative motive. Alice's refusal to go along with the "Lisa knows best" myth evoked a narcissistic rage in Lisa. She felt mortally wounded by Alice's difference of opinion, and it threatened her view of herself so much that she felt Alice must be her enemy. Ultimately, Alice had had enough therapy to know that Lisa was displacing onto her the earliest and most intolerable moments of her childhood, when she desperately needed the validation and affirmation that all children need, yet felt at a loss to repair the relationship with her fragile sister.

If we look back at some of the stories of the families who disowned children, parents, and siblings, we can see that in each case it was a response to an uncontrollable feeling of narcissistic rage that caused the need for the estrangement. Most often instigators of the estrangement are individuals who demand compliance and submission, coupled with an underlying feeling that if a family member is not submissive, that person is being disrespectful. The message the instigator perceives is that the nonsubmissive family member is treating him or her as if they were worthless. The excommunicator basically is saying, "You've made a life choice not because you wanted what you chose, but because you wanted to make a fool of me and humiliate me."

A client I'll call Maggie, a divorced woman of sixty, came to see me when her thirty-year-old son refused to act civilly and respectfully to her second husband. "When we married, Peter acted like a complete jerk, but he was in his early twenties, and Rob and I dismissed his behavior as immaturity. However, it's gotten worse over the years. Peter has a whole laundry list of complaints about Rob, and it's gotten to the point that we've totally stopped seeing each other or speaking because he's so unpleasant and angry around us. Unfortunately, his behavior is very similar to his father's, and that's ultimately why we divorced.

"The first few years after our divorce were OK, and, because Peter was still a teenager, the three of us often had fairly frequent occasions to be together, such as parents' weekend at college each year. My ex-husband's line was always that we were a happy and normal family, and when we were married, he had complete denial about how poorly we got along with each other. But before Rob was in my life, I guess Peter and his father could still pretend that we were this happy and normal family, and push the fact of our divorce out of their heads. I was shocked when Peter told me, after he met Rob and realized we had a serious relationship, "How can you do this to me? He's a creep. How can you be with such a creep? How can you even call yourself a mother?"

I explained to Maggie that Peter must have experienced her choice of being involved with Rob as a hostile act perpetrated against him, and perhaps against him and his father. They couldn't pretend to be a happy and normal family anymore, now that Maggie was making a new family with a new man in her life. "I've tried to explain to Peter over and over that first of all, Rob is far from a creep; he's good to me and he's a great guy and we have a lot of fun together. Beyond that, why would my being involved with a man be against him? It's plain nutty." "It's the busting of the happy family myth," I reiterated. "You took away Peter's ability to stay in denial, and he seems to feel that's unforgivable because of how badly it makes him feel about himself."

The Inability to Tolerate Mixed Feelings

People with an impaired sense of self have difficulty mourning, feeling sad, and tolerating mixed feelings. In order to harmoniously perpetuate any human relationship, we must learn how to balance our love and affection with our feelings of disappointment in the person we love. Most people accomplish this fairly easily and even unconsciously in relationships that are not "loaded," for example, with casual friends, distant relatives, and coworkers.

However, within the nuclear family, the situation is potentially explosive because of the intensity of the relationship. In other words, when a person with narcissistic tendencies feels these mixed feelings about a family member, he or she does not have the ability to accept a small level of disappointment in the loved family member. The disappointment then begins to outweigh the affection and positive regard, and the person begins to feel that the only possible solution is to extinguish that family member from the narcissist's landscape.

When parents cannot live with their disappointment that their child has created a life different from theirs, different from what they would have sought for that child, and all their attempts at creating the child they wanted to create have failed them, they often eventually feel the need to "bury" them. When siblings cannot tolerate their disappointment in a brother or sister, and their disappointment in the life-long relationship, that disappointment will eventually be expressed in persistent rage reactions which may very well culminate in a total severing of ties.

The people who are able to feel sadness, however, will, in response to a life transition that they find unsettling, become profoundly upset and unsettled; yet, over time they will be able to get over their hurt and disappointment with their family member's choice.

A healthy person who can tolerate mixed feelings will be able to let go of perceived insults and injustices, and let bygones be bygones. A person with an impaired sense of self, however, is unable to forgive or forget and will remain angry. This is ultimately caused by the black-and-white thinking of the person who struggles with an impaired sense of self, whereby they cannot say to themselves, "There is a great deal I dislike or even hate about my relative: his or her judgment, lifestyle, mode of self-expression, politics, values, religious beliefs, or sexual orientation. There is also much I love about this relative. We have a long history together. Much of it has been awful, but I can hold on to enough memories of the good times to live with my disappointment and sadness and let bygones be bygones." Healthy people can tolerate the dissolution of whatever myth they've lived with and move on in life. Injustice collectors, however, feel they need that myth perpetuated, that their very psychological survival is contingent upon perpetuating whatever myth prevents their self-worth from disintegrating.

The Inability to Tolerate Feelings of Envy

People with a profoundly damaged sense of self also are unable to acknowledge and get past feelings of envy. Roberta is a friend of mine who achieved great early success in the fashion industry and has always had enormous gratitude for her good fortune. Unfortunately, her mother and sister have envied her terribly and resented the fact that she has become affluent and well known, despite her best efforts to be generous to them. They've consistently responded to her generosity with contempt, disregard, and demands for more and have harassed her to the point of requiring her to seek legal counsel. Unfortunately, she's had to break all ties with them to protect herself and her children. Had her mother and sister felt satisfied with their lives, and not been plagued with pathological envy, they would have sustained a happy family relationship and been able to appreciate Roberta's success and willingness to be generous.

Janice, a therapy client of mine, enjoyed a good relationship with her family while she was in a bad marriage with a man who consistently cheated on her and spent money on cocaine and women while she worked two jobs. This was a man who also was remarkably similar to her father, and each of her parents seemed to find some comfort in that. Janice's parents lived close by and saw her difficulties, so they had no reason to envy her.

However, after she got into therapy, she left her first husband, married a man who supported her and was faithful to her, and led a comfortable and happy lifestyle. Her parents' envy of her caused increasing estrangement and iciness. Their envy of Janice's upward socio-economic mobility, and the fact that she was living so differently from her mother and with a man who was so different from her father caused them to withdraw more and more. It was as if Janice's good fortune was a way to make them feel bad about themselves.

If you're reading this book, most likely you are wracked with feelings that are untenable and unbearable for you to experience, and this is because you don't suffer from a character disorder. Your sense of self is sufficiently developed that you could live with your mixed feelings toward the family member who has banished you from their life. While the person with a character disorder always sees the fault in others, healthier people tend to suffer with self-blame and an impulse to mend the rift. That's what's brought you here: your ability to tolerate mixed feelings, your willingness to struggle with the dissolution of your myths and the changes in the homeostasis of your family, and your wish to mend the rift.

You, unlike the relative who has buried you alive, can experience others' choices as choices they need to make for themselves, and not as hostile acts against you to make you feel bad about yourself. You are eager to shake things up and create a new balance of power and way of operating with your family.

The Role of Homeostasis

According to family systems theory every family unit maintains a homeostasis within which the individual members' particular psychological states can be smoothly maintained. The homeostasis also serves to perpetuate the family myth. Rules evolve to sustain that myth and homeostasis.

When a member challenges the implicit set of rules, shaking up the homeostasis, and the family does not have the ability to negotiate conflict, a cutoff may ensue. When Janice remarried and felt safe with her new husband, she evoked the pathological envy of her parents and disrupted the homeostasis within her family. She dissolved the myth of the happy and close family and unfortunately saw that her autonomy was grounds for rejection. When Maggie defied the myth of happy and normal with her son and ex-husband, the new homeostasis for her family was an unfortunate one of estrangement.

Jason's coming out of the closet, Deborah's acknowledgment of her father's alcoholism, David's admitting his blended family was not a family that could get along easily with each other, Amanda's insistence that her mother stop telling her that she was brought up by a stay-at-home mother—all these are actions that broke through denial and disrupted the homeostasis of a family and generated a family cutoff.

Unconditional Love Can Allow for a Change in the Family Myth

In families like Maggie's and Janice's, yours and mine, any family that reaches an outcome of estrangement, there is an inevitable history within that family of a lack of unconditional love. Unconditional love, of course, does not include unconditional acceptance of unconscionable behavior, such as criminality or self-destructiveness or endangering the welfare of others within the family group. It does, however, include a notion that if behavior is within social norms, while there may not always be delight at a member's choices, nor approval, there is ultimately a stance of unconditional love.

While the Family Myth may decree that love is the regulating and driving force of the family, in fact, love experienced in the family that arrives at estrangement as a resolution is highly conditional. If it were not, estrangement would not take place. However, for love to be unconditional, a person's psychological development must be sufficiently intact to sustain assaults on self-esteem and to master separations and differences and changes in family composition necessitated by normal changes in life's events.

The Family Myth can be modified when, in fact, unconditional love does prevail. In the popular movie *My Big Fat Greek Wedding*, the father's fear of non-Greeks and his wish for his children to stay close to the fold, and not to deviate by marrying outsiders, is overridden by his love for his daughter, as shown by his ultimate acceptance of her marriage to a non-Greek. The myth in this family was so profound that the father's overcoming it touched the hearts of viewers and made for a cinematic triumph. It touched people's hearts because we all wish for that kind of unconditional love and support from our families.

This overview of the Family Myth provides what amounts to a stark blue-print. Some family members may be constitutionally incapable of giving up their adherence to the Family Myth they have created out of the fierce assumption that they can't survive without it. Other family members may prove to be more flexible and generous in their willingness to change the way they think about the family. The important point right now is discovering your own ability to change your way of thinking—to beckon to you, as you reflect on the ogres and angels, demons and saints in the myth to which your family may subscribe, to become perhaps the first *human being* in the "play."

A lot of your healing will proceed from that alone.

5

Learn from Successful Families

If we look closely at what I take to be the ingredients of a "successful" family (all of which contribute to a family that will stay connected over time), we will also see that these behaviors and proscriptions would *not* be well tolerated by the injustice collectors who cause a family to break apart. Pay close attention to the following list of successful family traits, and become alert to ways in which you may be able to embody these traits within your own family—if not your family of origin (if it's too late for that), then the family you have created or are creating for yourself today.

Successful Family Traits
- Autonomy is fostered; family members are encouraged to develop their own codes of conduct and governance, and they struggle to grant legitimacy to each other's thoughts and decisions.
- Independence of thought and action is permitted; people in these families feel free to make their own decisions without undue or permanent fear of withdrawal of love, affection, or positive regard.
- Individuation is encouraged; distinctiveness and uniqueness are valued rather than considered a difference or a betrayal. Even when a family member's uniqueness is upsetting or troubling, there is a determination to accept his or her distinctiveness as a human right.
- Communication and discussion are valued; there are ongoing attempts to foster contact and dialogue and to tolerate disagreement.

- Other people's feelings are regarded as important; they are heard and valued. Empathy for others is an imperative, even when this presents a challenge to family members.
- Family members attempt to talk to each other respectfully and politely, and when respect and politeness are breached, as at times they inevitably are, family members give and accept apologies.
- Birthdays, anniversaries, accomplishments, and other special occasions are acknowledged and celebrated, with an attitude of joyfulness and gratitude. Lapses of remembrance, while not sanctioned, are not treated as felonies.
- Family members attempt to freely and generously offer emotional support to each other, both during times of struggle as well as times of triumph.
- Family members value the empowerment of other members and attempt to aid and encourage rather than thwart or undermine other family members' power.
- Members strive to be nonjudgmental and noncritical, as they would hope others will not judge or criticize them.
- Family members attempt to mutually support self-worth and self-love rather than undermine and undercut.
- An attitude of generosity, warmth, and affection is the norm, while coldness, iciness, and miserliness are frowned upon. Feelings—even negative ones—are tolerated, and family members do what they can to understand and soothe each other's pain.
- There is tolerance for growth and development and the inevitable mistakes that people make, and family members are not subject to harsh criticism or brutal humiliation for making those mistakes.
- Family unity and loyalty to family members are important values within the family unit and take precedence over an individual's narcissistic concerns.

Unconditional Love

Families that successfully avoid estrangement and cutoffs live by a policy of unconditional love. This does not mean unconditional approval of all choices and acts in life, such as antisocial, criminal, or psychopathic behaviors. It does, however, mean that a parent or sibling or other relative does not make love conditional on submission to their needs and choices. Love is certainly not conditional on compliance with the family myth.

Michele, a client of mine who decided to marry outside of her Jewish religion, realizes she had experienced both conditional and unconditional love from two sets of parents. Her mother and father had divorced long before when Michele was a child, and both had remarried. While tensions were still high between her divorced parents, particularly from her father Jacob toward her mother Miriam, Michele had hoped both parents would ultimately approve her choice of spouse. Her mother offered that approval; her father decidedly did not.

In fact, Miriam wasn't thrilled with the choice her daughter was making, but her love for Michele was unconditional, so she felt motivated to find a way to work out her feelings about the marriage. She was able to value Michele's autonomy, independence, and individuation; she celebrated Michele's uniqueness, and she listened empathetically to Michele's needs. Ultimately, she learned to accept, respect, and value her daughter's choices. While she believed Michele might be making a mistake, she knew if that turned out to be the case, they would get through it together. (She certainly wouldn't be the first person in the family to make a mistake in their choice of marital partner, as Miriam could attest by her own history.)

Michele's father Jacob, on the other hand, loved his daughter conditionally. If Michele didn't pick a Jewish spouse, he told her, he would withdraw his love and the relationship would be over. He did not value her autonomy, her uniqueness, or feel she had the right to govern herself or make her own choices and perhaps her own mistakes. The component of his myth with which she was not complying was: "We all value marrying within the Jewish religion above all other considerations." This was more important to him than her wish to make her life take shape in a way that made sense to her and met her own spiritual, emotional, and familial desires and needs. It was also more important to him than his desire to maintain relations with his daughter and let her know that he still loved her. Michele's mother was able to put Michele's needs above her own disappointment since she knew it was, after all, Michele's life, and she loved her daughter no matter what.

This describes the essential difference between conditional and unconditional love.

"Different" Is Not Bad

Successful families are able to tolerate differences in choices among family members because they do not confuse different with bad. People who confuse different with bad regress to thinking like small children, who cannot integrate difficult, paradoxical, or unfamiliar ideas into their approaches to life without feeling threatened.

To some degree, we all do this. My wife, Cindy, and I were recently invited to the wedding of a friend's daughter; a young Jewish woman who was marrying a young man from Germany. Despite my rational knowledge that this young man had had nothing to do with the Nazi Holocaust, I found this young woman's choice of marital partner to be very unusual and unnerving, and I had some difficulty understanding how her parents had come to terms with the marriage. There was a part of me—a part of me I recognize now as the "small child" part—that felt that the marriage of a German and a Jew was quite "different" and therefore, somehow, inherently bad.

However, I managed to keep my primitive thinking and judgments to myself, and was in fact quite touched by how much this young couple clearly loved each other. I realized that World War II was long over, and that my task now is to accept who and how people are today. Perhaps the most dramatic proof that my old reflexive assumptions were wrong came in finding myself dancing the hora, holding hands with the groom's father who had been a soldier in the German army in World War II. I felt very grateful to have let go of a resentment that had no place at this wedding—or in my assumptions.

The Importance of Verbalizing Warm, Loving, Positive Feelings

Another characteristic of families that function successfully is that they have the capacity to say warm, loving, positive, and supportive things to and about each other. A client of mine who successfully completed therapy some time back, and came to terms with a permanent estrangement from his family of origin, worked hard to find ways to make things different with his own family. He came in for a single session recently, to discuss how to make a toast for the wedding of his son Ron. He said to me that as he started to write it, he had great difficulty expressing the warmth and positive regard for his son that he would like to express. "My father didn't even consider giving a toast at my wedding or my brother's wedding. It just wasn't in his repertoire to wax eloquently about how great his sons were. It was, however, becoming increasingly so in my repertoire, but doing it in public like this is really new. I really want to do it."

He later reported to me how great his son's wedding was and how pleased his son was with his toast. "Ron teared up as I spoke, and afterward he hugged me and told me how lucky he was that I was his dad. It was quite a moment for me, especially after all I went through with my own father."

Successful families are like any successful relationship; they are characterized by the expression of positive, loving, affectionate statements. Cindy's parents died when she was quite young but her aunt and uncle were as close as I ever had to a mother- and father-in-law. Her uncle died quite a few years ago, but her aunt and I are very close; we comprise a mutual admiration society that has allowed us to weather all kinds of crises and upheavals in the family. I always say I have the best mother-in-law in the world, and she counters with the fact that she loves me like a son. This is the kind of attitude and behavior that promotes enduring bonds and ties that do not break, even in the most trying times.

Negotiating and Sustaining Appropriate Boundaries

Functional families know how to create effective boundaries, ones that are not too rigid and not too fluid, and are respected but can be modified when necessary. Often the disputes that occur in families that become estranged relate to boundaries so rigid that they serve as barriers to communication of any kind, or boundaries that are so routinely invaded and overstepped that they create explosiveness, enmity, or ongoing disputes.

According to the *Oxford English Dictionary*, a boundary is "a thing which serves to mark the limits of something; the limit itself, a dividing line." Notice the absence of the word *rejection* in that definition? That's because boundaries—whether physical, psychological or emotional—are *not* rejections. They are, in fact, ways to live harmoniously with other people in mutual respect.

Families that function successfully can negotiate boundaries in ways that won't wound their members. "It was the most difficult task to get my sister to understand that when she and her husband came to visit from California that it was too much for us to have them stay in our Manhattan apartment during the weekdays," said Janet, a client of mine. "We take our vacations according to the school calendar, and they take their vacations according to their calendar, and we just can't take off from work when they're here, and we both work at home. Our guest room is my office, and it's just too disruptive to have guests during the work week.

"This offended my sister so much. She was so enraged with me, and went on and on about how hurt she felt, and how rejected she felt, and how she never would do that to me. (It's true she wouldn't, but she doesn't have a paid job and she has a large house with no space problem.) Anyway, we finally worked it out. I gave her all the dates a year in advance that I take off from work and stay in town, and also the days we're out of town and told her they're welcome to stay here then. I told her how much I love her and love hanging out with her and her family—which is true. I just can't have my space invaded when I'm working. I'm just not that flexible. That constitutes one of my boundaries."

The appropriate assertion of "what I am uncomfortable doing" or "what I'm comfortable doing" is respected by the members of families who succeed in nurturing each other—and staying together—over the long haul.

Successful Families Are Not Imperious

There is a famous cartoon that appeared in an English newspaper many decades ago of a baby being pushed in a baby carriage, wearing a crown on his head with the caption, "Make way for His Majesty, King Baby." That cartoon has been reproduced in some of the literature about recovering alcoholics to describe the psychological attitude of the active alcoholic, whose "entitled" imperiousness often causes him or her to trample on the rights and feelings of others. The infantile, addicted, narcissistic, borderline, or paranoid character who provokes family estrangement also assumes this kind of imperiousness, fashioning themselves to be, in effect, king or queen of a country that does not exist outside the realm of their own minds. In families that function well, there is no king or queen creating laws to which the subjects are subject; people who are adults in these families create their own laws, and others live with their decisions to the best of their abilities.

"The day I buried my husband was surely the worst day in my life," said Greta, "and the fact that my son-in-law Harry had to punish my daughter by not showing up at the funeral made it all the worse. I've never been a big fan of his; neither was my husband, but it's Cecilia's life and there's nothing I can do about it. I've got three wonderful children, and my other son-in-law and daughter-in-law are great, but now my husband's sister isn't speaking to me because she feels I shouldn't have let Harry back into my house. Well, I think that's crazy, and I've never gone off speaking terms with anyone. My sister-in-law's always got a list a mile long of people she feels should be punished, and when you don't go along with her edicts, she puts you right on her list along with her victims. I just don't see where it's my place to dictate to my grown daughter how to handle her husband, and I certainly don't think it's my sister-in-law's place to dictate to me who to let into my home."

Greta has good boundaries. Her sister-in-law has none—or rather, she has her own, and respects those of nobody else. Greta loves her daughter, but also knows she has no control over her daughter's marriage and how she manages her unkind and disrespectful husband. Her sister-in-law believes it is Greta's obligation to punish her daughter and son-in-law as if they are small children or subject to her unique laws.

A Successful Family Cultivates Empathy

The well-functioning family feels empathy for its members. When people have a capacity for empathy, they do not cut off a family member except perhaps in cases of severe abuse such as domestic violence. True empathy and a cutoff cannot coexist. I recently was consulted by a new client who came to me for help with a potential family estrangement problem. He and his ex-wife had agreed to share the expenses for their grown daughter's wedding. They had been divorced for many years, had a fairly amicable relationship, and in fact, prided themselves on being a well-functioning and blended family with their two grown children, his children from his second marriage, his wife, and her second husband. However, it was now three months since their daughter's wedding, and she was refusing to pay her share of the bill.

"I'm in a real bind now about this," he said. "She can well afford to pay, and I can't even imagine why she wants to take this stand. I know she's not thrilled with our daughter's marriage; she's moved clear across the country and God only knows how often we'll see her, but that's not my doing. I'm not any happier about that than Gloria, my ex-wife is. The thing is, now I'm caught between a rock and a hard place. I can afford to eat the $25,000 she owes me, although it makes me very angry. I can also take her to court for the money, and make a mess that will really hurt our kids. I mean, it would really be rough on them, especially for our daughter starting out marriage, to have her parents in litigation with each other. I think it's probably worth the money to me to just walk and keep my distance from Gloria. I think I just needed to talk this out aloud. She needs to create this wedge between us again for some reason; it was like this when we first divorced, and took many years to repair, I guess."

What is motivating this family man's decisions is finally an empathy and sensitivity to the greater good—to what will keep the family together as much as it can be kept together. His own distress is not his only motivation. His love and respect for his whole family supersede the distress and engender restraint in service of expressing his love for them.

A Functional Family Does Not Divide and Conquer

In our investigations of the injustice collector, we explored traits that overlap with those that characterize the borderline personality disorder, in which the person cannot see things except in black and white: there are no shades of gray. This leads to a reliance on a phenomenon called "splitting," in which people are perceived as all good or all bad. In families with borderline dynamics, splitting allows for frequent and deadly divide-and-conquer games between siblings. Children often become embroiled in competitive stances between "good child" and "bad child." When these feelings can be openly discussed and even joked about, they can be outgrown, neutralized, and not allowed to fester and become pathological.

My sons often joke with me that Jeanne is my favorite child; in fact, Jeanne and I are very close and we share many interests, and the reason the jokes are permissible in my family is that I believe they help my sons Steven, Kenny, and Ross express their aggression toward me and toward her in a healthy way. They also know fully well that I love all the children equally. Had I made a joke of that nature to my father, saying my sister was his favorite child, he would have taken it as a savage assault and become frighteningly angry with me for saying such a thing.

One family I know, dealing with conflicts between two sisters-in-law, provides another example of seeking out the positive in people, a trait which is central to any healthy family. Because these parents are *not* borderline personalities, they do not need to take sides and do not permit their grown children to play divide-and-conquer games. When their daughter complains about their son's wife, they simply say to her, "You have to do your best to look at her positive qualities and ignore her negative qualities and get along with her. She's your brother's wife and she's family." When their son complains to them about his sister's treatment of his wife, they simply say, "You know your sister doesn't mean anything bad with her behavior, and does the best she can. Tell your wife to do the best she can with her and try to get along with her. We love all of you and need you all to get along as well as you can. You don't have to be best friends. Just remain civil and be polite with each other."

Recently a close friend died, a woman who was the matriarch of a family to whom, when I was a teenager, I turned for the love and acceptance I didn't experience at home. Her daughter Jane and I had become friends at summer camp when we were sixteen, and for many years her home had become my second home. Her mom, Marilyn, and her dad, Harold, always welcomed their children's friends. They included anyone who wanted to be included and worked hard within their family to create an atmosphere of mutual support, love, and caring. They always had food at the table for whoever came in their house. All their four daughters' friends were always warmly welcomed, and treated with the same warm emotional generosity with which they treated each other.

Marilyn was critically ill for seven weeks, and during the time that she was in the intensive care unit, I marveled at how the four sisters and their families supported each other and avoided acrimony and disharmony. As a therapist, I had so often listened to people lament about the bitterness between siblings at stressful times and vent about the terrible things they felt their siblings did and said. I truly marveled at how wonderful the Keller girls were with and to each other and their dad.

At Marilyn's funeral, Jane delivered a very touching eulogy, and among other things, said, "Mommy would not tolerate any of us dissing each other or dismissing each other. Whenever we'd try it she'd just say, 'Aw, that's Amy,' or, 'You know how Alice is.' 'Stop it. You know how Emily is. You love her.' She always worked to keep us connected, and loving each other. . . . It was very important to her, and now we have something very special here. She spent all these years building it up, and we're so grateful to her for having the strength and courage to do so."

To live peacefully with anyone, a person has to learn to allow many remarks to go in one ear and out the other. A relationship is always bolstered when the negative is ignored or underplayed, and emotional energy is invested into building on positive statements, feelings, and activities.

Barbara, whom we met earlier, learned to feel quite comfortable over time with her estrangement with her sister Edna. At the same time, Barbara wanted very much never to become estranged from her own grown son Lawrence, whose wedding had provoked Edna's and Barbara's split. This was complicated by the fact that Barbara's husband and Lawrence had become totally estranged in recent years. It was complicated by Barbara's own reactions to Lawrence (and his wife), as well. Let me let her tell the full story—which, like most stories in actual life, follows some circuitous routes. Families have complications that breed complications. Here are some that Barbara has encountered, and her own account of how she used a healthy and mature self-restraint to keep from making them worse.

"On our last visit to Lawrence's he and my husband, Jonas, butted heads continually. They both are not very verbal, nor very patient, and each of them in his own way was quite abrupt and sometimes unpleasant with the other. Jonas came home and told me he was never going to visit Lawrence again, which is problematic given that it's quite difficult for Lawrence and his wife and our four grandchildren to travel here, and our apartment isn't big enough to accommodate all of them. Jonas knows how disgusted I am with him, and I've learned to live with how unhappy I am with him. However, I don't blame Jonas exclusively, and now just want to make sure I don't become estranged with my son.

"Lawrence is prickly like my sister and my father. He's quieter about it. He won't yell and carry on and tell you he's not talking to you again. He'll simply stop calling and won't respond to phone messages. Overall, he tries really hard, and he even tries to mend the relationship with his father, despite the fact that Jonas won't respond to him.

"It was my birthday last week. We were at my son Nicholas's house. We had celebrated my birthday with him and my daughter-in-law and my two grandsons. It was a lovely celebration, and I was really appreciative, and I was delighted when I got home and there was a lovely message on the phone machine from Lawrence. He said he had mailed me a gift for my birthday, and I realize a normal person would have been satisfied with that. At least I think so, but what would I know? I don't know any normal people.

"Now, I have a thing about cards. I *love* getting cards. I got birthday cards from my friends, my sister-in-law, Nicholas and his wife. I keep them out on the dining room table for a month sometimes, and I really love to look at them. But here I found myself listening to Lawrence's message, thinking how sweet it was, and then realizing he wouldn't send a card for my birthday; that for him, a phone call and a gift is enough, and I can only focus on not getting a card.

"Well, fortunately I know myself well enough to keep my mouth shut, because even I knew I wasn't being reasonable by expecting a card, too. When I did get him on the phone a few nights later, I kept my mouth shut about that, and simply told him how much I liked the gift which had come earlier that day. He then started to tell me how his wife was having all kinds of health problems, both physically and psychologically. Well, I know what her problem is. She drinks a bottle of wine every night, and she's clearly an alcoholic. Lawrence told me, 'I don't want anyone telling me my wife's an alcoholic. She likes wine with her dinner. That's it.' I knew from my time in Al-Anon that Lawrence couldn't and wouldn't hear what I was saying, just as when Jonas was drinking and I needed to be in denial, I would have said the same thing.

"My mother had had the same conversation with me about Jonas's drinking, and I still remember how horrible and ugly it got because she would not let it go. I hated her for that, and I think it made me even less willing to look at my complicity in Jonas's drinking. Fortunately, for me and my relationship with Lawrence, I had enough time in the program and enough therapy to simply walk away from him and not bring it up again."

Barbara is practicing almost all of what I think of as the ten fundamental principles of keeping peace in the family:

- She kept her mouth shut and did not express her provocative and negative thoughts and feelings.
- She vented her feelings by talking about her problems in therapy and Al-Anon.
- She didn't argue.
- She kept good boundaries and gave space.
- She didn't overreact.
- She stayed in the driver's seat. She stayed in control of herself.
- She used the principle of "what you see is what you get" in accepting her son for who he is.
- She focused on building up rather than tearing down, reinforcing for Lawrence how appreciative she was of the efforts he made, and she ignored the efforts she felt he should have made.
- She used her ability to empathize, putting herself in Lawrence's place, remembering the difficulties he had to endure growing up with her and Jonas and the dysfunction that went on in their family, especially when Jonas was drinking and she had not yet gone to Al-Anon.
- She also empathized by putting herself in his place as an adult, remembering how her mother attacked her for Jonas's drinking and it didn't help.

Families Promote Positive Feelings Through Sharing

Families that function well make great efforts to plan shared activities that will promote good memories—memories that build positive feelings. Strong families have regular traditions that are life-affirming and fun, and build bonds between members.

"My son and son-in-law's only shared interest is vodka martinis," Nancy told me, "and my daughter and daughter-in-law are only civil to each other as a gift to me. The four of them are really not very well matched. They've got very different interests, live radically different lifestyles, and have totally opposite political opinions. Fortunately, they all share an interest in good food, so twice a year we organize a family weekend at a resort with great food and lots of activities where we can all spend days doing what we want and we can share good meals in the evening. We've learned to avoid political discussions at all costs, and my husband and I work hard to steer the discussion to topics that are neutral, like wines, food, movies, plays, and travel."

I had met Nancy at a resort where I was vacationing with my family. I began talking with her when I noticed how she and her husband were interacting day after day with their grown children and grandchildren. She told me their history as a family had been rocky, and that she and her husband had to work hard to keep their family together. I asked her what she had meant about her daughter and daughter-in-law being civil to each other as a gift to her.

"I mean that very concretely. Those two are like oil and water. They just hate each other and are as different as night and day, although really they have nothing to fight about. A number of years ago their bickering was getting out of hand and they were at each other's throats continually and finally they refused to speak to each other. It was right before Mother's Day, and we had plans to go out for dinner and everyone was getting all worked up because Candy and Andy—isn't that ridiculous; they even have similar names—they weren't on speaking terms and how were we going to all be at the same table with Candy and Andy ready to tear each other's eyes out?

"So I decided to call each of them up, and I said to each of them, 'There's something I want for Mother's Day. I want you to cut this nonsense out and drop whatever it is you're angry about and get along with each other. If you love me, I want you to start speaking to each other. You don't have to be best friends, and you don't have to like each other. You just have to be civil and cordial and make it OK for us all to be a family and be in the same room together and enjoy a family holiday together. If you love me, you'll give me that for Mother's Day.'

"Well, it worked. I knew it would, because I put a lot of effort into my kids and grandkids, and they knew it was the right thing to do. I've had to do it a few times since then, but it's okay. I hope they'll learn from it and they'll use the technique if they need it once I'm gone so they can keep their families together too."

A Family Can Laugh

A sense of humor in a family is crucial: it can sometimes help to create bonds when nothing else can. One of my clients recently had great fears about coming out of the closet to his parents. A twenty-four-year-old college graduate, Derek had what might be considered a pathologically close relationship with his parents, who lived in the Midwest. He spoke with them almost daily, and had been kept awake nights fearing that his sexual orientation would destroy his parents, who, he believed, felt that he was a "perfect" child. Much to Derek's relief, his parents were unconditionally accepting, in fact relieved because they knew something had been bothering him, and his depression, silence, and reserve in recent years had been uncharacteristic of him.

In the weeks that followed, Derek reported an ongoing series of humorous phone calls between him and his parents. He'd tell them he was dating a doctor and about to make them the proudest Jewish parents in their town by bringing home an anesthesiologist. He'd ask his mother if the pink cake she made every year for his birthday meant she knew something she never told him about. The jokes and humor may not translate well here, but the point is, this was a family that needed to adjust to a major change and did so successfully using a loving sense of humor, one in which members gently and lovingly worked through their feelings of how to cope with the change in the family constellation.

A Successful Family Evaluates "Up," Not "Down"

There are issues and facts in life that are immutable; things over which we have no control. One of the key tools I borrow liberally from the twelve-step programs is the Serenity Prayer: "God grant me the serenity to accept what I cannot change, the courage to change what I can, and the wisdom to know the difference." One of the major tools for successful family harmony is learning to ignore the things we cannot change.

I talked with a woman recently who has worked hard to sustain a good relationship with her three adult children. "My middle daughter and I have always gotten along without a hitch. She's happily married and has three great kids. She loves the fact that I'm an involved grandmother, and she gets along great with my husband, and we get along great with her husband. There's never a problem.

"My oldest daughter is gay, and while I had some difficulties accepting it in the beginning, I've seen that she's happy in her life. She's doing really well in her career in biomedical engineering, but has had difficulties finding the right woman to settle down with, and I feel bad for her about that. She's in therapy and I'm totally supportive of her, and while we're not as close or in as much contact as I like, we do the best we can and enjoy whatever shared experiences we can figure out to have with each other.

"My youngest child, however, is a constant aggravation, and I must say, it takes a lot of work on my part to stay on good terms with him. I make great efforts to stay connected with him, and despite my efforts, he continually feels slighted and wounded by me, and also by his sisters. He's definitely a 'walking on eggshells' kind of person, and my husband and I and his sisters always have to work hard to stay off his bad list. I ignore a lot of the unkind things he says and use a mantra of keeping my mouth closed when he gets cuckoo with me. Fortunately, he and my husband share an interest in golf, so they can connect and share an activity when we visit with each other, and his wife, who's no walk in the park either, is a clotheshorse like me, so as long as we spend the day shopping, we do OK together. My son seems to do best when he has my or his stepfather's undivided attention; I know it's very infantile, but that's who he is, and it's worth it to me to gratify it as much as I can to stay on good terms with him."

A functional family has an implicit contract of forgiveness and letting go—a mature and benevolent attitude about overreactions and inappropriate responses during bad times. These are forgiven, and there's an attempt to evaluate the relationship up rather than down. Rather than remembering the ways in which family members were neglectful or hurtful, there's an attempt to connect with the ways in which family members are generous and warm.

One of the hallmark characteristics of the injustice collector is a remembrance of grievances going back years and decades. It's also a trademark characteristic of unhappy people. They are unable to forgive. Successful people and families are able to be contrite when they are in the wrong, and are able to forgive when wronged and move on and let go.

I talked with a friend who maintains a successful relationship with his aging parents despite his first marriage to a very difficult person. "I now realize my marriage to Sharon took two years not only out of my life, but also out of my parents' life. She had them so worked up, they almost didn't come to the wedding. Her demands, tirades, disrespect, and abuse were just awful. They pleaded with me not to go through with it, but I was stubborn and willful and wouldn't hear any of it. They were debating at the last minute whether or not to get on the plane to come to the wedding, and they decided they had to do it no matter what. They felt that I'd never forgive them and that I'd blame them forever.

"Well, within three months the marriage was over. She had some serious problems, accusing me of the craziest things and making unreasonable demands. Because I'm in business with my dad, she made completely extortionist financial demands. Between what she asked for, and the legal fees, and what we ultimately settled for, it cost my parents a lot of money. Anyway, they never once rubbed it in my face, never said, 'We told you so,' or 'You should have listened to us.' They were very supportive of my getting into therapy after that, and very happy when I met Angela and they saw what a good-natured and kind person she is. The fact that they forgave me my stupidity has made it easier for me to forgive myself and make a good life and marriage for myself now."

When I was a child, we used to say the Lord's Prayer each day in school. One of the lines in the Lord's Prayer is "Forgive us our trespasses, as we forgive those who have trespassed against us." The wisdom of this concept, found in many religions and spiritual beliefs, is that we cannot successfully live as long as we harbor resentments against others or ourselves. We'll look at the concept of resentment in greater depth in the next chapter, but for now, suffice it to say, the successful family does not sit with lists of injustices and crimes perpetrated by various family members against each other. Rather, the family moves on and lets go and, in the words of the twelve-step programs, lets God handle human transgressions. It evaluates up, not down.

Communication in the Functional Family

There is a range of communication permissible and even encouraged within a functional family that is prohibited in the family that ultimately ends up cutting off and becoming estranged from one or more family members. There is a freedom of speech that is modeled by parents and taught to children over time in a successful family, and it's learned as a way of life. However, when you've grown up in a family that doesn't allow this, you don't know much about freedom of speech.

Because of this, we need to get very specific about exactly what "freedom of speech" means so that you can begin to practice it in your attempts to build a functional family. Let's call it the "Family Freedom of Communication Act." Think of it as a new set of rules for membership in the family, especially given how poorly the old set of rules worked.

Family Freedom of Communication Act

1. Members can say how they truly feel when it will be constructive and will build a positive relationship; they can do this without fearing that they will stop being loved by other family members.
2. Members are guaranteed that they will not be shamed if they are honest and open about their feelings of hurt, loneliness, or rejection.
3. Family members will feel free to share inner feelings that they choose to share, no matter how unusual, abnormal, or strange their feelings are, because, after all, feelings are not actions, they are only *feelings*.
4. Family members are guaranteed that they will not be rejected by other family members if they let their feelings be known, again with the understanding that feelings are not actions, they are only feelings.
5. Members are entitled to the guarantee that they will not be made to feel stupid, ugly, ludicrous, or otherwise humiliated or put down for expressing themselves to other family members.
6. Members are entitled to assert themselves, and to have their self-assertion responded to either affirmatively or negatively, but not responded to with personal rejection or character assassination.
7. Members are entitled to a guarantee that expression of their feelings will not create a terrible mess for them in terms of their future relations with other family members.
8. Members are guaranteed that their feelings will be listened to and responded to in a way that they know they have been heard.
9. Members are promised that they will not be accused of being needy, greedy, or demanding if they try to talk about what they are feeling in relation to other family members.
10. Members are guaranteed that they will not be laughed at when expressing themselves.

The step we discussed in this chapter—learning from successful families—is important. You now have some concrete ideas and suggestions about not only what makes a "successful" family work, but also what you have the right to employ to make your own family work. This describes the goal of the rest of this book: to help make these new, positive family realities a part of *your* life.

6

Let Go of Resentment

"Living with resentment," so goes a memorable saying, "is like taking poison and expecting the other guy to get sick."

Resentment refers to the mental process of repetitively replaying a feeling, and the events leading up to a feeling, that goads or angers us. We don't replay a cool litany of "facts" in a resentment; *we reexperience and relive them* in ways that affect us mentally, emotionally, physiologically, and spiritually in very destructive ways. The inability to overcome resentment probably constitutes the single most devastating impediment to repairing a family rift or healing from the effects of one.

Although they may be provoked by recent, specific angry conflicts between two people, resentments usually encapsulate an enmity that goes much further back. Your sister may accuse you of a recent snub or slight ("How could you not have called me last week on my birthday?"), but the venom is more than likely fueled by years of other imagined or real snubs and slights, for which the recent accusation is just the trigger. The strong reaction of a resentment almost never appears to be warranted by what sets it off. It's always the product of a long history of backed-up unhappiness.

What causes the unhappiness that underlies resentment? We've already seen it laid bare in our discussion of the injustice collector's three obsessions:

- What we feel people did to us that was unnecessarily mean, hurtful, and thoughtless
- What people in our lives did not do for us that we feel they should have done
- When we feel the people in our lives have not done enough for us

Resentments embody a basic choice to refuse to forgive, an unwillingness to let bygones be bygones. When we hold on to resentments, we mentally relive all the injustices perpetrated upon us as if they happened yesterday. We review and rehash our painful pasts, even as we profess to want to let go of them. We do so because we have the illusion that by belaboring our resentments, we will finally somehow achieve the justice we believe we are due. We cling to a futile need to be right, which overrides the capacity to be at peace. We cling so hard to resentments usually because we don't know any other way of coming to grips with painful feelings of hurt, rejection, and abandonment.

We need to learn to let go of resentments, because living with resentment can only bring us chronic punishment and pain, and prevent us from building up loving, nurturing, and supportive relationships. Clinging to your angry, hurt, and outraged feelings about family members will only hinder your capacity to move on in your life and learn to deal with the wounds. Letting go of your resentments, whether it leads to healing the rift or to wholeness and peace within yourself or both, is thus integral to not letting your family rift rule every day of your life.

Fortunately, there *are* ways to get out of resentment's crippling grip. In this chapter you'll learn about alternative, more life-affirming and healthful responses that will help you achieve freedom from them—choices that you may not realize are available to you.

Poisoned Mind, Poisoned Body

Let's take a look again at that quote: "Living with resentment is like taking poison and expecting the other guy to get sick." This makes vivid one of the most crippling aspects of resentment—one you may be experiencing right now, reading this book. If you're still struggling with feelings of rage, sadness, and disappointment, thinking about ways to get even and prove to a family member that you're right and they're wrong, you know this—especially when you realize that the family member who is the focus of your resentment may be feeling just fine, enjoying life, and perhaps not at all troubled by any of this. Resentment hurts you far more than the person you resent.

Resentment can become a black cloud that prevents us not only from seeing the good in other people, but also the good in our own lives, in ourselves.

It can prevent us from engaging in the life-affirming, productive, and interpersonally satisfying activities that are available to us.

So what's the payoff in a resentment? Why do we cling to it? One reason is physiological. Resentment changes us chemically, pumping adrenaline, making us feel more fully aroused, hearts beating faster, breath quicker. Charged and ready to go to battle, we wake up in the middle of the night thinking about our "enemy," ready to do battle with the monster that really is only in our minds. There is a kind of fierce aliveness in resentment: it may give us a momentary sense of justice and purpose. But the toll is great. It ultimately drains us of any possibility of serenity, composure, and ability to feel peace.

I've struggled with resentment and forgiveness as I sought ways to cope with the estrangement from my own family, so I understand how difficult a process it can be. At one point, I was at a restaurant with my wife and children and some friends, when a group of people sat down at the next table. Among this group was an elderly man who might have been my father's identical twin. Instantly and without awareness, my mood went from festive to foul. I suddenly felt enraged, stopped enjoying the company and the meal, and began to obsess silently about the injustice of how my father has treated my family and me. Looking back on it now, I might as well have been eating dinner with my rejecting and abusive parents rather than my loving and accepting wife, children, and close friends.

I've learned over time to manage these reactions more effectively, and contain them more quickly. Now I can stop myself from getting lost in these states, and I feel much better about myself, but I am aware, always, of what a difficult challenge it can be. I know firsthand just how hazardous and hurtful my own resentment can be to me and the people I love.

How have I learned to get out from under these toxic feelings? How can you? Take the following suggestions to heart and you'll already be on your way.

Ten Steps to Letting Go of Resentment

1. Approach resentment as the addictive state of mind it is.
2. Realize that you are using resentment to replicate your family drama and maintain a connection with those dramas, a necessary acknowledgment before you can let them go.

3. Examine how your resentment may come from mentally confusing people in your present life with people in your past.
4. Acknowledge that you cannot control those who have rejected you.
5. Recognize that your resentment gives you only illusions of strength. Instead, highlight and validate your *real* strength and power.
6. Learn to identify the signals that provoke resentment.
7. Practice cognitive behavioral techniques to stop indulging in resentment. Put a thought between your feelings of resentment and indulging in ruminating about them.
8. Acknowledge your part in allowing the abuse to occur, forgive yourself for that, and make a decision to not let it occur again.
9. Declare an amnesty—with your family and with yourself.
10. Forgive when you can, and practice willful and deliberate forgetfulness when you cannot, keeping in mind that these acts are gifts to yourself rather than capitulation to those whom you resent.

Treat Resentment like Addiction

Resentment is like addiction in many ways, not the least of which is that both are physiologically as well as psychologically toxic to us. Once we indulge in either, it's quite difficult to let them go. Just as recovering alcoholics know that 'one drink is too much and a thousand not enough,' once we allow ourselves to indulge in resentment, we get lost in an insatiable hunger for revenge, endlessly reviewing the many incidents that we feel prove our enemies' ill will and malevolence.

Our biological systems react and respond to this state as they do to drugs or alcohol, and a primitive, unconscious aspect of our brain controls our thinking as well as our bodily response. The biochemistry of the process is not relevant to our quest to eliminate this dysfunctional behavior, but if you are contending with a family that cuts off, you've undoubtedly entered this territory and experienced it: the adrenaline rush and high of enumerating how badly you've been treated and all the ways you plan to get even.

A wealth of medical studies have shown that holding onto resentment and an incapacity to forgive will cause blood pressure to go up, weaken the immune system, and provoke cardiovascular degeneration. Refusing to forgive, or at least forget, floods the body with stress hormones that cause symptoms ranging from headaches to colds and flu, impaired circulation, premenstrual tension, fatigue, irritable bowel syndrome, anxiety, migraine, fibromyalgia, and other stress-related afflictions.

The Adrenaline Rush of High Drama

Let's look at how a couple I worked with learned to acknowledge that holding onto resentment was a way to create a high of sorts—an adrenaline-fueled rush of drama and excitement that, despite their avowed and conscious wish to avoid it, was just too intoxicating to stop. Then we'll see how they found a way to get out from under the grip of this drama through a different kind of self-reflection.

Matt and Jeanette came to see me for help with an ongoing rift they experienced with Matt's parents, whom they hadn't seen or spoken to in over three years except for several dramatic ugly episodes.

"It all centers around our children's birthdays and Christmas," Jeanette told me. "They always hated me, from the minute we got engaged, and Matt just doesn't function well when he has any contact with them."

Matt added some details about his family, to show me that Jeanette wasn't exaggerating. "My family is really nuts, and they all go on and off speaking terms with each other continually. The only time I ever got along with my parents was the three years my dad was in jail for income tax fraud. They pretty much had to be nice to me, since I was supporting them after the government froze all my parents' assets. Once that mess ended, their shenanigans began again. It's not just them. It's my mother's whole family, which is basically ruled by my wealthy grandfather, and the scenes and ugliness that go on between my mom, her sister, and her two brothers, and now everybody's adult kids is hard to believe. The only one we're able to get along with now is one cousin who also doesn't have contact with the rest of the family."

One way Matt's parents would provoke contact with Matt and Jeanette was by sending gifts to their young children. Matt and Jeannette weren't in contact with them and were put in the difficult position of deciding whether or not to accept these gifts—especially since their four- and six-year-old daughters have no relationship with their grandparents and can't even remember ever seeing them. "The first Christmas, I decided I didn't have the right to not give my daughters the gifts, and I wrote thank-you notes to Matt's parents in their names," Jeanette says.

"Well, this seemed to make Doris, Matt's mother, think she was entitled to see the girls, and she had the nerve to call me and suggest I drop them off at her house for a visit. This was about six months after she had started an actual physical fight with me, ended up pulling my hair and telling me I was a whore who was driving her son away from his family. I told her I wouldn't allow them to be with her unsupervised, as I felt she was out of control. Well, this just set her off and we started another screaming match, after which she told me to return the gifts if she couldn't see the kids. The problem though was that she had bought the girls gifts they really liked.

"The next day, in a complete rage and consumed with thoughts of how I would get even with Doris, I went to Toys R Us and bought the same toys new and had them shipped to Matt's parents. I also added a nasty gift card telling Doris exactly what I thought of her. Once again, I was so aggravated and enraged, Matt couldn't tolerate listening to it, and we ended up in a huge fight."

Matt jumped in: "I wrote them a note telling them not to send any more gifts to my daughters, that the only gift they could benefit from was having grandparents who weren't completely psycho, and since that would clearly never happen, they should put the idea that they had grandchildren out of their mind altogether. I should have known it would provoke another crazy response, which it did in the form of a phone call from my father threatening that he was going to report us to the Bureau of Child Welfare as being abusive parents.

"Well, that made Jeanette completely insane, and we had yet another huge argument until I could reassure her that a threat like that from my family meant nothing—that they always did stuff like that and would never follow through on it. That ended it for the moment, but each birthday and Christmas, there's a new episode. We just need help in learning to manage it."

As I continued to work with Matt and Jeanette, I learned about Jeanette's childhood and family. She revealed that her relationship with her parents now was much different than it had been during her formative years. "My Dad was an alcoholic and real wild man throughout my childhood. There were knockout drag-down fights between my parents, bottles being smashed, the police would come, other relatives would be called to get involved; there was always big-time action.

"A few times my Mom packed up my brother and me in the middle of the night and moved us into her parents' house, and as often as she said she wasn't going to put up with it anymore, she was madly in love with my dad and he'd win her back. Anyway, when I was fifteen, my dad quit drinking and became involved with AA, and my Mom started going to Al-Anon. I'm not even sure how it happened, or why it happened then, but life in my house became radically different from that moment on. My parents are great now and the picture of warmth and stability, but it certainly wasn't always like that."

Matt and Jeanette continued to look at how they together mismanaged and mishandled Matt's parents, and saw how they allowed them to create the adrenaline-fueled high drama that was reminiscent of each of their childhoods. They each talked about the fact that they wanted their daughters to grow up without the misery of ugly drama and family feuds, and that had led them to the conclusion that if Matt's parents couldn't act any differently, they would need to break off ties with them. They also each talked about and acknowledged a secret part of themselves that loved the drama and how the adrenaline rush of these scenes and battles with Matt's family had them feeling a kind of high.

After exploring these issues of maintaining connection with each of their families—for Matt his present-day family, and for Jeanette, the family of her childhood—they came in for a session after their Christmas holiday. They both were grinning from ear to ear as they entered my office. "We received gifts for the kids in the mail right after you left for vacation," Matt told me. "I guess the work we've been doing here has really paid off, because this time we knew just what to do. Before taking the gifts to the post office to send back to them, I sat down and wrote this note to them, and now three weeks have gone by and they finally have left us alone." Matt showed me the note he composed:

> *We thank you for thinking of sending our children Christmas gifts, but after careful thought about all our best interests, we feel it is better for the girls, for us, and for you if we do not accept any more gifts from you. We don't need a response from you, and I'm sure, you, like us, will feel better if you don't burden yourselves with a response. Thanks again.*
>
> MATTHEW

"Instead of the drama of an ugly fight between us and a series of insane phone calls or letters exchanged with Matt's family," Jeanette said, "we ended up going out for a wonderful dinner and seeing a movie, and I have to tell you, it's much more satisfying watching the scary drama on a screen in the comfort of the movie theater than it was being the stars of our family horror show."

Handling Resentment like a Drug: Choosing Abstinence

Resentments, like the ones Matt and Jeanette are now learning to give up, are horribly pointed and specific—they can shoot into you like lethal laser beams. Examples: "I was up all night last night fuming about what my son said to me, calling me a bum and failure. I feel just awful today; it's like having a hangover." "I got myself so worked up thinking about how my daughter-in-law insulted my wife and me that I became afraid that my blood pressure was going out of control." "I worked myself up so much about an abusive phone call I got from my sister that I ended up in bed with a migraine." "Whenever I think about my sister's alcoholic husband's final tirade at me, I just lose myself in the whole history of abuse from my family and can't stop thinking about it until I collapse in exhaustion."

If these ultimately self-lacerating statements ring a bell—if they're anything like what keeps you up at night—then you need to learn to make a resolve similar to that made by recovering addicts: abstinence. It may not at first sound as simple as deciding not to take a drink or not to gamble. It's so easy for a situation or person to trigger resentment, and so hard not to go off and running with it. However, if you make the effort to remind yourself daily that this is a harmful addiction, you can learn to stop your behavior. As we move on in these steps, we'll learn more about how to recognize your triggers—the first step in refusing to react to them in the old ways. We'll also discuss specific steps to stopping self-destructive thinking.

How to Stop Using Resentment to Replicate Your Family Drama and Maintain a Connection with Them

We've looked at how the roles we play in our families serve to enact longstanding, often replayed scripts and dramas. When a family cutoff takes place, we're left with a void: the script we're accustomed to performing—in the absence of other characters—makes the dramatic dialogue a toxic monologue. Sam was a client who came to see me because of his estrangement with his mother, who did not accept his wife because she was Hispanic. Sam told me about a scenario that plagued him—even though he was determined not to actually carry it out.

"My mother had always wanted me to be more conventional, less artsy and intellectual, less left-leaning politically. This conflict began when I was in high school.

"I grew up in an affluent suburb of Cleveland, and from the outside, my family looked like the American Dream. Dad was successful, Mom was pretty and active in charity work, and my sister and I were great students. We went to church every week. From the outside, it all looked great, but behind closed doors, it was crazy.

"My parents couldn't stand each other and at the rare times my dad was around—business trips took him away repeatedly—they'd fight constantly. Mom never cared much about anything other than how my sister and I looked—if we looked good, that was good enough for her. She spent most of her time at our country club or involved with things like the Junior League, pretending to care about the charities for which she helped to organize parties. Dad made a lot of money as an attorney, traveled as much as possible, and when he was home, he disappeared to his golf club.

"I was supposed to follow in my dad's footsteps, be a jock in high school and go on to Ohio State and law school, but that just wasn't me. I gave up track and basketball in high school because I preferred being in the Drama Club and acting in plays, which didn't please my parents at all. When I joined the school's Lively Arts Club, my father actually gravely asked me if I was gay. I did go to Ohio State, but instead of going on to law school, I went and got a degree in international business, and, while working for an American firm in Mexico City, met and fell in love with Rosa.

"Shortly thereafter, Dad died, and when I went home for his funeral and talked to Mom some days later about my plan of becoming engaged to Rosa, she said, 'I'm not having a gold-digging Spanish whore in my family or my house. Ever.' I assumed she was simply suffering from some temporary insanity because of my father's death, so I decided to ignore her ugly statement. When I told her Rosa had a great job in the same firm as me, and she came from a very wealthy family, Mom told me that she must just want to marry me to become an American citizen. I decided to ignore that too and once again figured her abrasiveness must be reflective of my bad timing on the heels of Dad's death.

"After Rosa and I were engaged, I called Mom and asked her to come down to Mexico City to meet Rosa and her family. Her response shocked me: 'I have no interest in going to Third World countries, and if you've decided to lower yourself and marry outside our race, I really can't imagine that I could have much to do with you.' I just blew up at that point and told her I wanted nothing to do with a bigoted, judgmental, critical old crone such as her.

"Then I called my sister, who had spent her whole life following the pre-scribed plan and was married to a guy who was a young associate at my dad's firm. Suzanne and I had never been terribly close, but we also had never clashed particularly either. When I told her what had transpired between our mother and me, I got my second shock of the day. 'You must understand how Mommy feels, Sam. How would it look to bring a dark-skinned woman to the club, after all.' Well, that was pretty much it for a relationship with my biological family. We exchanged letters and phone calls for a time, some accu-satory, some more conciliatory, but ultimately my mother never changed her position and my sister turned out to be a clone of our mother.

"Rosa and I had a wonderful wedding in Mexico City and relocated to New York two years ago. Now she's pregnant, and I couldn't be happier, but I can't get my mother and sister out of my head. I keep playing out this fan-tasy in my head of going back to Cleveland with Rosa, and going to Mom and Suzanne's country club with her, and making a huge scene to embarrass, mortify, and pay them both back for the horrible way they've treated me and their refusal to accept my choices. Of course, I would never do this; the last thing I like is a public scene, and frankly, Mom and Suzanne would only use it as more evidence of my always doing the wrong thing.

"The thing that really bothers me is that I have different versions of this little drama going on at different times. And I waste a lot of energy coming up with them. There's the one where I show up in church with Rosa, and another one where I go to my dad's old firm, upset Suzanne's husband, and hope he takes it out on her. Sometimes I imagine getting me and Rosa pro-filed in one of the local papers so everyone in town will know we're sane, good, and respectful people, and Mom and Suzanne must be horrible people to have cut us off.

"Each time I come up with versions of this scenario, the dramatic dialogue goes through slight script changes, but each time I come up with different crushing lines to deliver to Mom that I hope will destroy her. I don't think this is good for me, but I don't know how to stop it. I also know Mom is impervious to heartfelt feelings and totally convinced about the rightness of her choice, and no matter what I did or said, it wouldn't matter a bit."

Sam and I spent some time in therapy talking about how his ongoing drama was a replay of what life must have been like for him every day growing up. He realized he had never quite come to terms with how different he was from his family of origin, and how bad he had felt about himself because of this. He talked about many times that he reached out to his mother, and was summarily rejected and cast aside. He remembered how weird he always felt hearing his parents' bigoted statements, and heartless reaction to news stories about tragedies that befell any of the many groups and types of people they disliked.

Sam realized that his frustration level at the end of his mental dramatic replays was as great as the frustration he felt every day of his life while he lived with his parents and sister. He said, "I always felt like an outsider in that house. I think that's part of the reason I loved being in school so much. Other kids celebrated when school was on vacation, but I cried because I had to be at home or go to that awful, stuffy country club. It's funny. I didn't feel like an outsider during the day, especially in high school once I got involved with other kids who were more like me, and now my life is great and I never feel like an outsider. It is nuts that I keep replaying this scene where I end up feeling like the outcast—unaccepted, judged, criticized—when in my actual day-to-day life, I'm fortunate enough not to ever feel that way."

As Sam understood more and more how he remained connected to his family with his chronic replay of his resentments toward his mom and sister, he also talked about the pain of never having had an accepting, loving family, and how much it hurt to have been cut off by them totally. He also came to terms with the fact that most likely, his children would never know their grandmother, and he and his mom, with whom he rarely had a good minute, would most likely never reconcile. He also discovered that there were concrete tools he could use to stop the annoying chattering going on in his brain all the time, and, later in the chapter, we'll go through some of these methods.

Stop Confusing People in Your Present Life with People in Your Past

Leslie is a client who talked with me about her ongoing difficulties with her son's fiancée, Robyn. "From the first time I met my daughter-in-law, we both felt awkward with each other. That was apparent to my husband Barney and to my son Neil. When Neil asked me what I thought of Robyn, I said to him 'I'm sure as we get to know each other we'll become great friends,' but in my heart of hearts I had my doubts. When Barney asked me about my reaction to Robyn, I told him I couldn't stomach her, and I didn't know why, but I was sure I'd manage to get through it; after all, our son loves her.

"When I married Barney, my parents and especially my mother tried to tell me what a bad choice I was making, and they made our engagement and wedding a nightmare of a time. I was in love and I really didn't want to hear what they had to say, and it built terrible resentment over the years that never really got better. We had brief periods of doing well with my family, followed by terrible feuds and periods of estrangement. Gradually we all learned to settle into a cordial and amicable peace with each other by having very infrequent contact, and the only reason that worked, I think, was that Barney and I consulted with a good therapist about how to deal with them.

"Their dire predictions that Barney would be an awful husband and that we'd end up divorced proved incorrect, as we have been happily married for thirty-two years now. The problem is I want to say the same terrible things to Neil as my parents said to me, and as the wedding draws closer, and Robyn and her family show their obnoxiousness—in my opinion at least—I find it more and more difficult to hold my tongue. More than that, though, it's obsessing on all this that consumes me and drives me crazy. In my head, I make lists of all Robyn's faults and tally up any and all evidence of what a deficient character she is. It's driving me crazy, it's hurting my marriage, and it's not fair to my two younger children, who must realize that I'm on another planet a lot of the time."

Leslie began weekly sessions with me, and, as she had done in the past, talked about tools to manage herself when she had contact with Robyn and her family. Over time, she also talked about her parents, particularly her mother, who she realized had been rejecting, devaluing, critical, and cold to her for her entire life. One day she came into her session and told me she had a dream about Robyn.

"The dream doesn't make sense to me," she said. "My issues with Robyn are about how she's not talkative, not inquisitive about me, doesn't really want to get very close to me. She's definitely not a 'touchy-feely type,' and I find myself frustrated by her formality with us. She and her mother make all the decisions about the wedding, and it bothers me that they don't solicit my opinion, but since they're paying for it I tell myself they have the right to do so. Anyway, in the dream, I was showing Robyn the dress I had bought for their wedding, and she was devastatingly critical of it, of me, of my taste, and told me I would stand out like a sore thumb if I wore that hideous dress to the wedding. I got very upset and tried to defend myself, but the more I did that, the more coldly critical she became. I woke up in a rage and then felt completely confused."

"What confused you?" I asked.

"Well, the one thing that Robyn does that makes me happy is she always compliments me on what I'm wearing, and asks my opinion of clothes. She says nice things about our home, and asks my opinion about her bridal gown. One of the only good things I can say about her is that she seems to value and respect my taste and sense of style, so I don't really understand why the dream took the form it took."

Suddenly Leslie's mouth dropped open and her face brightened, and she exclaimed, "Oh my God, it's my mother. My mother was the one who always had something negative to say about the way I dressed and the way I looked. That's who the dream was about. We fought about what I was wearing to school every single day of my childhood. This battle continued through the last weeks of her life when, as sick as she was with cancer, she always had a nasty critical remark about my clothes or my hair, or implied I was gaining weight or aging poorly."

As Leslie and I continued to explore this new and deeper understanding of her reactions to her future daughter-in-law, she began to realize that, in reality, there were many similarities between Robyn and her mother. Like Leslie's mother, Robyn was not an outwardly warm person; both of them had a way about them that Leslie, at least, experienced as cold and distant. Unlike Leslie and most of the people with whom she felt most comfortable, her mother, like her future daughter-in-law, was reserved, self-contained, not terribly inquisitive. Because of Leslie's experience with her mother, Robyn made her feel very anxious.

"People like Robyn always push my buttons," she explained, "and I anticipate an attack and get very nervous. Robyn, in fact, unlike my mother, has never attacked, but it's as if I'm waiting for her to do so, and I get busy preparing a defense ready to use against her. The more I do this, the more I feel resentful toward Robyn for behavior that's actually only taking place in my ever-overactive brain."

I pointed out that Leslie was unconsciously confusing Robyn with her mother, and responding like the helpless little girl she once was rather than the strong accomplished woman she had now become. The impact of this understanding had an immediate benefit. Now, when Leslie feels this old resentment—which she now knows has nothing to do with Robyn, and everything to do with her mother—she is able to cut it off at the pass. "There just isn't any reason for it now," she says. And she is a little freer than she was before.

Acknowledge That You Cannot Control Those Who Have Rejected You

When we indulge in resentments, we become like the police chasing a criminal, and then like a prosecutor trying to present a case to the judge. Yet all our efforts aren't effective. By mentally rehashing our resentments, we are attempting to control our own emotional pain and hurt, as well as the behavior of those who have hurt us. The problem with this, however, is that we have no control over either our pain or the behaviors of others in our lives. In fact, the more we try to control our feelings by reviewing and ruminating about our resentments, the more out of control we're bound to feel. We become trapped in a cycle of resentment and loss of control, much like the addiction cycle of a drug addict or alcoholic.

"I've found that the only thing that stops me from obsessing about how awful I felt after my mother committed suicide when I was sixteen, is to become consumed about how enraging it is that my father cut me and my brother out of his life six years later," says Stefan. A successful television producer, he has lived through one of the most painful family estrangements I've ever heard of.

"Ultimately," he tells me, "they both made the same choice, which was to resign from being our parents, and in each situation, I had absolutely no control. I'm someone who likes to stay in control, and with each of my parents, I've had to admit I was powerless and had absolutely no way to make things different. My mom has been dead for many years now, and my dad, from what I hear, is remarried and living with his wife and her two teenage daughters."

I asked Stefan how he's learned not to be consumed with his feelings about all this rejection and abandonment. "Ever since I can remember, my childhood was about taking care of my depressed mother and learning to stay out of my dad's way. He was a violent and abusive guy, always in a rage, and never really acted like a father in any normal sense of the word. The good news is he didn't stay at home much, and when he was at home, if you stayed out of his way, he'd forget he even had kids. He just wasn't part of our lives, and Mom, I guess, did the best she could given how messed up she was. Dad made enough money that we didn't have to worry about a place to live or having enough food to eat, and Mom was too feeble to do more than try to stay out of his line of fire herself.

"I think overall I didn't really have a childhood in any conventional sense of the word, and realized early on that if I wasn't a fighter and ferociously hard worker that I was going to end up as wretched as I perceived my parents to be. By the time my mom killed herself and my dad cut us out of his life, it wasn't very strange to be, in effect, orphaned. When each of those events occurred, I felt consumed with upset, rage, and feelings of how unjust life was to me. Mom's cutoff from us had a finality that left me with a futile rage, and Dad's cutoff ultimately evoked what felt to be an even more impotent rage, because he was alive but I knew he had never really wanted to act like a parent to us anyway.

"Every time I think about either of them, I start to feel out of control, and if I'm not careful, that feeling gets worse and worse. Years ago a friend who's a recovering alcoholic was telling me about AA's Serenity Prayer and how useful it is to him when he feels out of control. He wrote the prayer down for me, and since then, when I start to feel that way, I silently say the prayer to myself: 'God grant me the serenity to accept the things I cannot change; courage to change the things I can; and wisdom to know the difference.' That calms me right down."

We encountered this prayer in our last chapter. We see in Stefan's case that its effects go deep if you can really register each component of it—acceptance, courage, and wisdom—and understand the greater task, which is to be willing to let them in.

Learn to Recognize Your True Strength and Power

Phyllis was a survivor of the terrorist strike on the World Trade Center on September 11. I admired her courage and determination to carry on with her work at her company's new location just one week after the terrorist attacks. She spearheaded the reorganization of her company and their continuing operations in the face of relocation and the loss of many valued coworkers who did not escape. She responded to the expression of my admiration by saying, "I've always done what needed to be done," and I then speculated that she must be no stranger to trauma.

She said that actually she'd been lucky and blessed with a relative lack of trauma, at which point Jonathan, her husband interjected, "Who are you kidding, Honey? When your crazy parents, brother, and sister refused to come to our wedding, and cut us out of their lives completely? You don't consider that a trauma? I remember it was devastatingly traumatic for you."

Phyllis laughed and said, "Oh yeah, I guess so. My crazy parents decided Jon was not a suitable husband for me and for no reason other than that they disliked anyone my brother, sister, or I became involved with. That was pretty much the end of any relationship with my biological family. I guess you'd consider that a trauma."

I asked her how she got through that one.

"Well, OK," Phyllis sighed, as she began to remember what had happened. "I guess it was a trauma. In fact so much of one that I was devastated at first—emotionally paralyzed. It was unthinkable to get married without my family there, without my father walking me down the aisle as I'd always imagined.

Then I got angry, and I worked myself into an even bigger rage when my brother and sister backed my parents' opinion and indicated they also were done with me if I married Jon.

"Soon my family was the only thing that was on my mind. I wasn't sleeping, eating right, taking care of myself; I was oblivious to Jon and my work; and I became obsessed with thinking of ways that I'd make them all pay for this unjust treatment. I've always taken pride in being a strong, driven, and determined person, and I've been successful at doing almost anything I set out to do, with the one exception of getting respect, support, and validation from either of my parents. Whenever I was around them, I felt weak because no matter what I did, they remained critical and rejecting.

"Somehow, Jon managed to snap me out of it simply by telling me he missed the strong and loving woman he had planned on spending the rest of his life with. He also pointed out to me that in the year we had been dating each other, my parents had done nothing but devalue me, give me grief, and been cold, distant, and unwelcoming to him. He reminded me how supportive they were to my thirty-two-year-old sister who still lived with them, and my thirty-four-year-old brother, who, he felt, either lived a secret life or had no life other than his job in the same company where my dad works.

"Anyway, somehow it felt that Jon took the shackles of my family off me, and I decided Jon and I would make the most wonderful wedding, and make our wedding day great despite their boycott. I saw that all the strength I was using to think of ways to get even with all of them and prove to them how wrong they were about Jon, could just as easily be used to plan a wedding, as if I didn't have parents—or any living family, for that matter. Rather than thinking about ambushing them and forcing them to be the people they never would be, I decided I could use my energy to creatively plan a newly conceptualized wedding party.

"Instead of the catered wedding in the grand ballroom I had always imagined, we got married at a friend's country house, under a beautiful spring twilight sky, and then had the grandest picnic with Jon's family and all our friends. Southern fried chicken and potato salad and some cases of wine and champagne later, it was the most fun wedding banquet anyone had ever attended. It was wonderfully unique and unconventional. Jon's brother and our best man walked me down the aisle, and I never even thought about my family's absence."

We can see how Phyllis converted her futile and consuming resentments into refueling her mind and aims, using this energy for creative rather than destructive purposes. We saw a similar accrual of strength and power for Matt and Jeanette when they were able to use their real strengths to manage Matt's family rather than fuel the flames of the family feud. This rechanneling seems to come only when you recognize the uses to which you've been putting your negative energy and acknowledge the considerable power your resentments are draining from you. This recognition is painful, but a necessary step before you can free yourself to rechannel your energy. With practice, you'll learn you can rechannel your energy more and more at will: resentment's toxicity does not have to consume you. You can then start to operate from your real strengths, not the illusory strengths of revenge scenarios.

Learn to Identify the Signals That Provoke Resentment: HALT

We need to look at both the internal and external factors that can lead us into the obsessive and toxic state of resentment. Again we can turn beneficially to a tool used in all the twelve-step recovery programs to help people prevent relapses into addictive behaviors. And resentment can certainly be called a kind of addictive behavior subject to relapse. It is crucial to recognize the signals that lead to our relapsing into resentment and to take steps to ameliorate the distress that these signals represent.

Many people in twelve-step recovery become familiar with the acronym HALT, which can encourage you to be vigilant about recognizing states of mind and body that might easily lead to relapse:

- Hungry
- Angry
- Lonely
- Tired

I've found in my own situation that it helps me to be vigilant about HALT, and to take appropriate actions when necessary. "Hungry" and "tired" signal to me that the *body* is important—keeping it regularly nourished and rested is a big part of the task of helping me to know serenity. "Angry" and "lonely" are emotional states of which I've learned to be wary, as well. They can shoot straight into resentment if I don't take steps to assuage my momentary feelings of isolation or frustration. When any of us experiences the discomfort or deprivation of a HALT signal, we are always more vulnerable to obsessive ruminations and indulgence in resentments. Meet your needs for healthful food, rest, companionship, and peace before you even attempt to assess or understand anything to do with a family rift. It's a kind of internal housecleaning that I've found absolutely crucial to gaining a healthier perspective about anything.

The next thing you need to do is evaluate your personal "hot spots"—to use another twelve-step phrase, "people, places, and things" that set you off—and learn that they can be used as danger signals to cut you off at the pass of resentment, rather than as matches to the flame of it. (Leslie learned from the work she did with me about her future daughter-in-law how self-contained, quiet, withdrawn, and reserved women are a hot spot for her.)

Here are some common hot spots to be wary of:

- Having unstructured time
- Alcohol
- Drugs
- Bosses
- Coworkers
- Holidays
- Depressed people
- Boredom
- Teachers
- Being taken by surprise
- Being around people who are drunk
- Male authority figures
- Female authority figures
- Being criticized
- Being praised
- People who invade my boundaries and personal space
- Silent, uncommunicative people
- People who get needy
- People who overdramatize

- Hysterical, overreactive people
- Workaholics
- Laziness
- Being asked to borrow money or possessions
- People who think too highly of themselves
- People who are self-effacing and self-devaluing
- Careless people
- Fastidious people

Like most addictions, indulging in resentments is also a solitary activity. It precludes genuine connection to others and genuine interaction, and ultimately can crowd out all other relationships within a family. When people speak to others of their resentments, it's rarely a mutual exchange of ideas or a dialogue; it's most often a diatribe, and one in which the resentor seeks complete agreement rather than dialogue or support or feedback. When the focus of family gatherings becomes one of rehashing the various diatribes and accusations of the injustice collector, those diatribes and accusations are given that much more power.

April came to see me to find ways to reduce her dysfunctional connection with her family, which was currently in chaos because of an ongoing battle between her father and her brother. April's brother Alan has a long list of grievances against their parents, particularly their father, Abe. Abe has in fact acknowledged and affirmed the validity of some of his son's accusations, and has apologized in an attempt to make amends with Alan. Alan, however, insists that his father has neither sufficiently apologized, nor expressed his apologies in a sincere enough manner. He refuses to forgive his father, has held onto his resentments toward Abe, and will not speak to him or be in the same room as him. He is also not speaking with April because she is not taking his side in the argument and has not complied with his demand that she stop speaking with their parents as well.

April reported having had dinner with her parents on a recent weekend, and told me what a good time they were having, when her father suddenly launched into how frustrated and upset he was about Alan's attitude toward him. "Bringing up Alan's name in the middle of a pleasant and happy dinner is like being on a beautiful beach on a sunny day, and all of a sudden the clouds move in and a torrential rain and thunderstorm makes everyone run for cover. We all get tense and upset, and lose ourselves in a discussion that leaves us more frustrated than ever.

"I've decided I'm not letting Alan rain on my parade anymore, and I just said to my parents, 'Let's not go there. It's not going to go anywhere good; we're not going to solve the Alan problem, because that's up to Alan. Can we drop this now before we all get sick to our stomachs and go back to talking about real life and all the good things that are going on?' It was great," she said. "My parents actually heard me and it made sense to them and we went on to enjoy the rest of the evening."

April has learned that Alan's behavior is out of her control, and she's tried to teach this to her parents. It's helped that they've also gotten therapy and talked about this and have realized they've done all they can to heal their rift with Alan. She's learned to use the cognitive therapy techniques we talked about in Chapter 1 to reframe her thinking about this subject, and consequently to change her behaviors. She's also learned that an injustice collector who holds on to resentments and lives in a state of toxic rage can cause her to act the same way, and has decided she's no longer going to allow her brother to induce this kind of behavior in her.

April's role in the family had been that of the people pleaser, always trying to appease and go along with Alan in order to avoid disharmony. She's learned that for her to live in a state of serenity and feel healthy and whole, she's got to stay away from her own resentments—evoked by a person, Alan, who is clearly determined to live in a state of resentment.

Acknowledge Your Part in the Creation of the Resentment

Throughout this book we've witnessed the pain and anguish of people living in resentment. I have personally struggled with resentment, and seen how letting go of resentment can both mend a family, as it did mine in 1991, or help me to move on when my family couldn't mend our rift in 2001.

Let's go back to 1991, when, after years of feuding with my family, my father announced on Thanksgiving morning that he was done with us. My sons were three and five years old, and it broke my heart to think of them not knowing their grandparents. Beyond that, it felt unbearable to think of having a living family but becoming indelibly estranged from them. Sure, I had heard of this happening many times and worked with a number of patients for whom permanent estrangement was a reality, but I just couldn't imagine it happening to me and Cindy and our children.

Cindy and I were fortunate in our professional knowledge, and neither of us could accept the status quo as it existed that dark fall of 1991. Cindy's parents had died many years before, and my parents were the only grandparents our children would ever know. We managed to separate ourselves from the problem sufficiently to realize that the ongoing lists of resentments that my parents and also the two of us were carrying around with us at all times formed the biggest obstacle to creating family harmony. We knew this from our clinical work with both couples and families. No interpersonal relationship can move forward in a positive way when people are busy looking backward and trying to prove the righteousness of past complaints.

Cindy and I were able to create the conditions that allowed for mending the relationship by first acknowledging our part in the ongoing family feud that had been taking place. We realized we were culpable for having sometimes behaved provocatively. Indeed, we'd provoke or we'd allow my family to treat us less than respectfully, and, for the sake of peace in the family, ignore much of their behavior that we didn't like.

We never really thought about this too much or worried about it, but when the family feud escalated into full-blown estrangement and we gave this a great deal of thought, we realized that we had responded to my family's aggressive and provocative behavior in kind, by our own offensive and thoughtless behaviors. Once we realized this, we had to forgive ourselves and treat history as a learning experience, resolving not to act this way in the future. This essentially laid the groundwork for the next step, which was to ask for a family-wide resentment amnesty.

Declare an Amnesty

Frankly, we both experienced the idea of permanent estrangement as unacceptable, shameful and awful beyond belief, and we knew, given the personalities of my parents, that it was up to us to mend the problem. We were, thus, prepared to bend over backwards not only to keep the peace, but also to try to increase positive feelings between us, to become more loving, and to beckon to my parents to "put away their resentments . . . and disappointments" as we were putting ours away. We were ready to declare an amnesty on old wounds and hurts, and we hoped they were ready too. I put it this way in a heartfelt letter I wrote at the time:

> *Dear Mom and Dad,*
>
> *Cindy and I are both very saddened and discouraged by our recent estrangement. We've talked at great length about this problem, and realized that both the two of you and the two of us have long lists of resentments, anger, injustices and disappointments which should be forgotten and put aside. As far as we understand from our experience, the only way to have a relationship with each other is to put away and stop discussing the hurts and resentments of the past.*
>
> *We plan to follow this course, and to try to build a future based on a positive and mutually respectful basis, enjoying shared interests and experiences to the extent that we can all manage. We know that your list of resentments and injustices are as extensive and lengthy as ours, and equally painful to you as they are to us. We hope you'll be able to follow the same course, and move into the future with a forgetting of the past.*
>
> LOVE,
> MARK

Happily, both my parents and sister were willing to follow our suggestion of letting go of resentments and building a future as a family. We managed together this way for the next ten years, with difficulties but maintaining an overall level of amicability—apart from a few isolated episodes when one or the other of us could not help expressing at least a little anger at my parents' or sister's occasional outburst or insensitivity. Cindy and I managed to set good limits that warded off their provocations, and we managed to control our own behaviors. I'm sure there were instances where they also found us provocative and managed to control their reactions and let go and move on.

Forgiveness and Resentment

The dictionary definition of forgiveness is "to cease to feel resentment." However, when a family member responds to our attempt to make amends for some behavior by not accepting those amends, and not reciprocating with amends toward us, we may simply feel we can't forgive. Each of us must be his or her own guide here: we may sometimes not be able to forgive someone who has wounded us badly and repetitively.

Yet, whether or not we forgive, we still need to take steps to clear our minds of obsessive overinvolvement with others' transgressions. Forgiveness has to do with the relationship between you and the person you may feel has hurt you: you may or may not be able to grant it, depending on the severity of that hurt. However, in either case, you can let go of *resentments*, whose only real function is to keep us in a state of poisonous, negative, angry, and rageful all-consuming thoughts about a past we cannot change.

There is much discussion in our society today about forgiveness and the psychological and spiritual benefits of clemency. I believe firmly that life is better when people can forgive each other and move on in their relationships. However, when forgiveness is not merited, it's still possible to find a place for our feelings that will not consume us or plunge us into a state of toxicity.

Religious leaders of many faiths advocate forgiveness, as do health care providers citing the extensive cardio-vascular and immunological benefits of doing so. The Dalai Lama said, "I believe one should forgive the persons who have committed atrocities against oneself and mankind," yet he went on to caution about the importance of not forgetting. "But this does not mean one should forget the atrocities. One should remember these experiences so that efforts can be made to check their reoccurrence in the future." A similar attitude prevails in Christian theology, when we look at the Lord's Prayer and say the words, "Forgive us our trespasses, as we forgive those who have trespassed against us."

Whether we forgive or we don't forgive, the fact that remains consistently clear from the perspective of mental health is that we need to drop the *resentment* in order to feel healthy, whole, and fully alive.

Toward Wisdom and Freedom

Letting go of resentments starts you on the path to greater wisdom—not only about the effects of a family rift, but about everything in life. Getting free of resentments is the only way to be and feel truly free and unshackled, because as long as we're burdened by resentments, we are imprisoned by those whom we resent. I've learned in recent years that I can decide to be angry with someone I love, without having to share it with them or treat them as poorly as I feel they're treating me. It's a tremendously liberating proposition to accept those we love for who they are—including the stuff that exasperates us—and focus on what we love about them.

7

Make the First Move: Learn and Employ Active Measures to Reconcile with Your Family

N ow that you've given yourself the very precious gift of starting to let go of your resentments, you're in a great position to attempt to mend the fences between you and your family, if that's the right move for you. Just as you learned to give up your resentments as a reward to yourself, as opposed to seeing it as giving in to a bully, mending the split with your family can also be a gift to yourself. If you can manage it, it's much better than the illusory pleasure of being "right"—a very questionable triumph that inherently breeds loss.

The odds are that you're contending with a situation similar to the one I was facing with my family in 1991. Here we were, two factions, each saying the exact same thing to each other: "You have hurt me to such a degree that I am no longer willing or interested in having any kind of relationship with you." Whenever this kind of situation occurs, if a reconciliation is to occur, someone must initiate it and put him or herself into a leadership position to mend the rift. If you feel you are ready and willing to take on this kind of job (as I was in 1991), here is the five-part plan toward family healing I recommend. We'll fully explore each point in this chapter.

- Look closely at yourself and your behavior. Make a fearless inventory of the negative traits you need to temper and control to improve your relationship with your family.
- Stop taking the inventory of your family's faults.

- Declare an amnesty and see if it's accepted.
- Do a needs inventory to find ways you can better cement the relationships with your family.
- Creatively plan shared experiences as building blocks for a newly defined relationship.

Looking at Yourself and Taking an Inventory

Start by looking at yourself, and thinking about how you could manage your family in a kinder, more loving, and more generous manner. Acknowledge what you do to provoke family disharmony, and resolve to change those behaviors. As we discussed in earlier chapters, in our families we learned to act out a particular drama.

We've followed a certain script while playing a prescribed role, and we've done this probably since we became part of the family, that is, way before we had any ability to make a conscious choice about what "role" we might really want to play in the family. It's axiomatic that if we keep doing the same old thing, we'll keep getting the same old horrific results. New behavior begets the possibility of brand-new outcomes—outcomes that can have some very beneficial surprises.

Zip It

Learn that you don't have to say everything you feel, and that you can take the time to frame feelings that you need to express diplomatically. This is an important tool and most of us use it in many areas of our lives. In fact, outside your family, you more than likely already possess the skill to take a moment to reflect after the feeling hits about what appropriate action to take that will best serve your purposes. You probably do it at work when you deal with coworkers or supervisors, in a store when you get frustrated by a clerk, and in any social situation with friends or acquaintances during which you feel a negative emotion. You automatically remind yourself, in these instances, that expressing your negative feeling is probably not in your best interests, or if it's absolutely necessary that you do so, you'll go to the lengths of framing it in a diplomatic and self-protective way.

With our families, however, we've often learned to "let-'er-rip" and not think as carefully about the consequences of what we're saying. Thus, often, families bring out the worst in us. Adults at these times can quickly regress to immature out-of-control children in response to parents, brothers, sisters, or even our grown children. These eruptions are the seeds that plant family rifts, and when they occur frequently enough, ultimately can be guaranteed to ignite the fuse leading to total estrangement.

Your neighbor's daughter may come to visit you with her newly dyed purple hair, and you easily refrain from telling her that she looks ridiculous. However, when it's your daughter, you feel free to immediately let her know exactly what you think of her outrageous and idiotic hairstyle. Some daughters can tolerate this; others cannot. If you know your daughter can't, begin to practice diplomacy. You'll know you need to do so in order to be able to continue living civilly and harmoniously with your child. On the other hand, if you're the daughter and your mother is the one who can't hear a request to keep her comments to herself, you can learn to simply say you can understand how she feels and are sorry she feels that way. You can keep your family relationship running more smoothly this way, as opposed to telling her she's a hypercritical, meddling witch and the cause of every minute of unhappiness you've ever had in your life.

When my family cut us out of their lives in 1991, Cindy and I each decided to look at how we contributed to the alienation and chronic strife, and how we had our share in the repeated family feuds.

"What do I do to create or inflame the problems with my family?" is the first question you need to answer for yourself if you are looking to ameliorate a family crisis. This does not mean that you are the source of the problem, but the only behavior you have any guarantee of changing is your own. Look at the following checklist and take note of those areas of behavior that you may need to work on to end the feuding with your family. It is a list based not only on my own experience but that of many patients who, when they became ready to acknowledge their own complicity in the family rift, saw that there were some very helpful concrete actions they could take to begin to heal it.

Acknowledging Complicity in the Family Rift: Behaviors to Change

1. I speak my mind without first thinking through the consequences of what I am saying.
2. I am quick to express my anger and hostility toward my family.
3. I say provocative things that I later regret.
4. I forget other family members need recognition, attention, and my interest in their lives.
5. I forget important occasions, such as anniversaries and birthdays.
6. I have trouble listening to other family members and really trying to understand how they feel. I am quick to argue with them rather than listen to them.
7. I do not make clear the boundaries I need to sustain family relationships.
8. I ignore or violate boundaries that family members have requested me to keep.
9. I fight every possible battle, rather than ignoring the small stuff and reserving my battles for important concerns.
10. I overreact at times when I really could exert greater self-control.
11. I judge others too quickly or harshly.
12. I stick to a policy of never giving in and never admitting when I am wrong.
13. I persist in feeling and acting disappointed and angry with family members who I know are probably never going to be different. I refuse to accept the fact that "what I see is what I get."
14. I persist with futile attempts to change members of my family when I know that they will never change essentially because they don't want to change.

A Fearless Inventory

There are many tools you can employ to overcome and change the above list of behaviors. Denise came into treatment to repair a rift with her mother-in-law. "I'd actually be fine with never seeing the woman again as long as I live," Denise told me, "but she is my husband's mother and my children's grandmother, and because I love them, I want to learn to manage her more effectively.

"My husband is an only child and has always been the apple of her eye, and she's felt from the day we started dating that I've come between them. I finally realized that when I allow her to provoke me, I give her what she decides are grounds to stop speaking to me. That means she has succeeded in coming between my husband and me. He ends up angry with me *and* with her, and we end up fighting yet again about her. That gives her what she wants: to be as present in our lives as she can be, even if it's as a wedge between us. If I can stay out of the fight, I'll end up winning. The way I respond now, I always lose, and we—my husband and I—always lose."

Denise worked with me on developing various deflection and avoidance techniques to deal with her mother-in-law. She had a busy life being a mother of two school-aged children and holding down a full-time teaching job, and thus had additional incentives to stop wasting her time negotiating ineffectively with her mother-in-law. I suggested to her toward the end of one session a homework assignment of creating what twelve-step programs call "a fearless inventory" of her own behavior and the ways in which she made the problem worse with her mother-in-law. If she were willing to do this, she would find a new clarity and develop far more effective strategies of dealing with the family mess she was in now.

This notion of an inventory is spelled out in the fourth of Alcoholics Anonymous's twelve steps—that to create profound change, a person must become aware of the full panoply of his or her character traits, both good and bad, strengths as well as weaknesses. Taking the inventory can be seen as an exciting and rewarding challenge—a whole new means of self-exploration and discovery. It amounts to putting on a new pair of glasses, one that may allow you to see yourself and the effects of your actions more clearly than you ever have in your life.

One good way to approach this task is to make a list of the character traits that you dislike in the family member or members from whom you're estranged. Next, add traits you dislike in those whom you have, at best, mixed feelings about. Then see if any of those traits apply to you—and see if enumerating them suggests further traits you have that they do not. Think about unpleasant characters in books you've read and the qualities of the bad guys in movies you've seen. Do you see parts of yourself in any of them?

With time and effort, you can come up with a comprehensive list of liabilities in your character or personality that you can control. But the assets part of the list is important, too. Once again, focus on your family members from whom you feel estranged and itemize their positive qualities. These may also mirror your own positive qualities—and, again, suggest others that might not have occurred to you until you began making this list.

Denise came up with her own comprehensive list by the next week and showed it to me in her therapy session. "In a way, this wasn't so difficult for me," she said. "I teach high school English and specifically creative writing. I'm always working with students on being as specific and to-the-point in their written narratives as they can be. So I didn't hold back with my own specifics here. The difficult part was the rude awakening it meant for me— especially my realization that family members I'm angry at really do bring out my worst traits! Especially my mother-in-law."

Look at Denise's inventory of negative traits in the following list and see if it can provide a kind of hunting ground you can use to find possibly similar traits that apply to you—with which you can create your own fearless inventory.

- Stubbornness
- Argumentativeness
- Defensiveness
- Intolerance
- Impatience
- Irritability
- Guilt-mongering
- Rigidity
- Perfectionism
- Self-righteousness
- Self-pity
- Whininess

Creative Tools of Behavioral Change

Once Denise had acknowledged the character traits that she wanted to tame, control, and abstain from, she was ready to go to work to find creative solutions for doing so. That she was a creative writing teacher again provided an advantage. She was highly responsive to the idea that she could, in essence, rewrite the future course of her relationship with her mother-in-law—in a sense, treating their painful past dealings with each other as something that needed editing. The creative solutions Denise came up with enabled her to heal her family rift—and brought her to closure in therapy with me as well. Three of them center on learning to escape conflict before it has a chance to take hold and escalate:

1. Creative Prevention

"Phone calls are the easiest way to manage her," Denise says she realized. "Before, when she said something provocative, like criticizing how I bring up our children, I used to start to defend myself, which only provoked nastier and more critical comments. This would escalate until I blew up and said something I regretted. Now I've learned to tell her there's someone on the other line calling long distance, or that the smoke alarm just went off, or that one of the kids is calling for me and I'll call her back later.

"I don't really like lying to her, and lying doesn't come naturally to me, so I've learned to tell myself that I'm doing creative prevention and somehow that makes it more OK for me. I then wait to call her back at a time I'm sure I'll get her voice mail, and I can then say, 'I'm sorry I missed you, hope you're well, and let's talk soon.'"

2. Change Course

"Another way I've learned to get out of a conversation that's going to lead to a blow-up is to put one of the children on the phone and tell them to tell their grandmother what they did in school that day," Denise says. It's what she calls "changing course by whatever means necessary." "My kids are in second and fourth grade, and I know my mother-in-law, as much as she does love her grandkids, has very limited tolerance for their little school-day tales, especially when she's in a mood to pick a fight with me. It's almost a sure-fire method to get her off the phone. Of course sometimes my kids engage her, and talking to them helps break her bad mood and urge to lambaste me."

3. *Pay Compliments*

"In person," Denise continues, "my mother-in-law is more challenging, and usually the best method to shield me from her fighting mode amounts to capitalizing on her vanity. She's a very narcissistic woman, and puts great effort into pulling her wardrobe, make-up, and accessories together in a way that she thinks makes her look beautiful. Frankly, I think the only thing that would make her look better is to put a paper bag over her face, but again I've learned to apply my creative prevention solutions to tame the shrew. I'll tell her how gorgeous her new ring is, how great it goes with her earrings. I'll ask her the name of that new shade of nail polish, and tell her that her pantsuit is the most stylish outfit I've seen in ages.

"She always goes for that bait for a while, and as I'm dishing the flattery out to her, I'm actively multitasking and scanning the environment for escape routes. If we're at my house for dinner, it's easy because I can always find something that I have to do in the kitchen, and she never wants to go into a kitchen under any circumstances. If we're at a larger family gathering, I'll bring another person into the conversation and then subtly slip away. Wherever we are, there's always the bathroom as a last resort, and if I'm really at wit's end, I can suddenly come down with a terrible stomach virus that prevents me from being anywhere but in the bathroom or in bed. It's active, hard work, but I am getting different results.

"She loves to fight so I'm sure she's fighting with someone else. I don't know who she's fighting with now, maybe one of her sisters or one of the women in her bridge club. It doesn't really matter. The more I stop her from provoking me and consequently creating a rift between us and then between me and my husband, the more I feel I win, and that's better for all of us. I'd sum it up in this way: either I stay distant and dodge the bullet, or I jump in and let her destroy me. I can't give an inch, or she'll take a mile."

What You See Is What You Get

Looking at your own behavior and letting go of past resentments are great starts. In order to build a future, however, you have to stop thinking about what you don't like about your family. It becomes imperative that you learn to accept the members of your family for who they are, no matter how much you may like or dislike them.

Taking other people's inventories is also a cause of brain fatigue, in that no matter how much you think about a loved one's faults, inadequacies, insufficiencies, and failures, you will not motivate that other person to change his or her character. Dwelling on your family members' failings simply encourages you to *keep* dwelling on them—with no payoff of change. Learning not to take another person's inventory is like learning the truth of the old lightbulb joke: even a hundred psychoanalysts cannot change a lightbulb that doesn't want to.

Personal change can only come from within. As much as we would like a family member to stop drinking, start being thoughtful, stop nagging, start talking about his or her feelings, stop criticizing, be less self-involved, or change whatever else he or she may be doing that's driving you crazy, we cannot expect to change others' behavior for them. Indeed, nobody can change another person. With great effort, we can only change our *own* behavior—which gives us our only hope of moving on. This also means accepting the principle of "what you see is what you get."

Jill had come to see me several years ago and had finished her treatment some time ago. However, she still comes in sporadically to address various concerns when she needs a sounding board, or a reminder of options available to her, especially to help her cope with members of her family. She started therapy initially because her father stopped speaking to her. After we worked together to learn tools to attempt to repair the relationship (which her father had resisted), I helped her accept his decision to write her off. Later on, after the father died, her sister similarly wrote off Jill and her brother, and like their father, was intractable in her decision.

Jill came in recently because she needed help managing her relationship with one of her two grown children. "Garret's always been difficult and prickly, and actually very similar to my father and my sister," Jill told me. "He was my father's favorite grandchild, and continued to be in touch with his grandfather after my father had cast me out of his life." Garret, she reported to me, now has three children of his own and is "becoming more like my father all the time." Brian, her husband, was barely able to tolerate being in the same room with Garret. Garret had further exacerbated family tensions by recently telling his brother, Jeffrey, who accused Garret of being arrogant and disrespectful, to "drop dead and forget he ever had a brother."

"Like my father, Garret could not tolerate anything that smacked of criticism. He has always been convinced that he's been wounded by other family members, and never has been able to acknowledge his part in creating the strife. Jeffrey ignored Garret's treatment of him for a long time, and when he told me after their last fight that he wasn't going to apologize this time for not being willing to live with his brother's disrespect, I couldn't criticize Jeffrey for his decision.

"I can see that as Garret gets more overwhelmed in his life that he acts more like my father and reacts to me and his father in ways that are upsetting, to say the least," Jill continued. "I don't think I'm overly critical or overly demanding as a mother or a person, but increasingly Garret responds to me with outbursts of anger and impatience. If I say anything whatsoever about his behavior, the outburst becomes positively hostile and abusive, and recently escalated to the point of stating, 'I've had it with you, and with Dad too. I'm done'—he spelled it loudly: 'D-O-N-E—with both of you,' and slammed the phone down.

"I know him. If I don't pick up the phone to call him, he'll just never see me or his father again. He won't necessarily demand an apology from me so long as I don't ask that we discuss that awful phone conversation. My husband won't initiate any contact with Garret. He's just fed up. So I know it's up to me. Garret's my son, and I am determined not to be estranged from my children, as my father was with me. I just need help in learning how to deal with him and avoid these blow-ups leading to estrangement."

I talked with Jill about needing to accept Garret for who he is, and living with the "what you see is what you get" principle. We had talked about it in the past, and I reminded her of how she had used it to get along with her husband and her demanding and critical supervisor at work. We discussed how she had managed to let inflammatory remarks go in one ear and out the other. We talked about how painful it was for her to accept that her son was such an abrasive individual, and how upset she felt that her two children wouldn't talk with each other.

After we discussed these things for several sessions, Jill said to me, "It's sad to have to relate to anyone in such a careful and guarded way, and the fact that I have to relate to my own son with the vigilance of walking through a minefield is even sadder. But I'm going to have to do it, because the alternative of estrangement from him is even sadder still. Whatever it takes, I have to accept him for who he is and learn to live with him as he is if I want him in my life. And I do. He's my son and I want him in my life."

Declare an Amnesty and See If It's Accepted

Just as you declared an amnesty when you worked on letting go of your resentments in the last chapter, this next step you're taking involves suggesting an amnesty with your family or family member. Again, this involves giving up the "who's right and who's wrong" battle and a willingness to stop playing the blame game with your family so that you can move on in a new way. If just one person in a dispute is willing to proceed into the future with a clean slate, his or her spirit may be reciprocated by other family members who are equally eager to mend the fences but simply lack the tools and self-understanding to do so.

Gillian and Edward have consulted me intermittently over the years for help in dealing with Gillian's family, one with a history of major feuds followed by periods of varying lengths of estrangement. They were particularly troubled over the ramifications of this for their two young sons, who were getting confused as to why they sometimes had grandparents in their lives, and sometimes didn't. Their most recent feud was over Gillian's acceptance of her lesbian sister Carolyn, an acceptance that her parents couldn't manage. They felt that her continuing to have a relationship with Carolyn and Carolyn's girlfriend was tantamount to betrayal, and for the last three years had been estranged from both their daughters.

On September 11, 2001, Gillian and Carolyn each received their first phone call in three years from their frantic parents. They were especially frantic because the last time they had been in touch, Carolyn had been working in the World Trade Center, and they weren't aware her firm had moved. "Somehow that phone call was all either of us needed. We talked about it and we could hear in their desperate voices that despite their cutting us off, they loved and cared about us a great deal. Given what was going on in the world at that moment, we all seemed able to forgive and forget, and since then, by and large, we've done OK."

Sometimes it takes a tragedy to repair a family relationship. A friend of mine who was estranged from his family some years ago also told me that a tragedy had repaired his relationship with his family. He had been estranged from his parents and two older sisters. When his one sister was diagnosed with a brain tumor, and his mother called him for the first time in years, he also reported a desire to declare an amnesty. He was devastated by the news, realized he loved his sister, and was ready to forgive and forget the various hurts he had been previously unable to forgive.

Other times an amnesty can be created via the initiative and leadership of a strong family member. Sylvia and Frank came to see me about how to repair the damage done by their alienating their daughter for marrying outside of their race and religion. They talked with me at great length about how regretful they felt about their behavior when their daughter Dawn announced her engagement to Andre, an African-American, and at the same time how they only recently began to understand the reasons why their son-in-law, then their daughter's fiancé, had accused them of being racist.

Two years had gone by, and Sylvia and Frank recently heard their daughter was pregnant. They still had difficulty with Dawn's marriage, but had come to realize that they had even greater difficulty with the estrangement. Though they also had great difficulty with the notion of having a biracial grandchild, they had even greater difficulty with the idea of not knowing their grandchild.

Sylvia and Frank acknowledged that in the Jewish Eastern European immigrant homes in which they had both grown up, there had been a great deal of racial prejudice, and an overall negative attitude toward anyone of a different religion, let alone a different race. They now acknowledged their son-in-law was accurate in calling them racist, even though the delivery of his accusations was rather poisonous. Also, on a trip to Europe, they had recently encountered anti-Semitism and prejudicial treatment for the first time in their lives. They understood better why their son-in-law and daughter had been so angry with them, and now wanted help in rekindling the relationship.

"Our last contacts with them were over the phone, and they were awful. Dawn and Andre were terribly volatile, as I remember it," said Sylvia, "although I'm sure we didn't handle the situation well and weren't even aware of how bigoted we sounded. Now we've tried to call to apologize and ask them to let bygones be bygones, but we're afraid of rejection and not having the ability to explain to them how we feel we've changed—and changed for the better, and are regretful about our past behavior."

After a few sessions of exploring different options, Frank and Sylvia came up with the following letter to their children, which did allow, ultimately, for the relationship to move forward with a clean slate:

> *Dear Dawn and Andre,*
>
> *We can't begin to tell you how much we regret our behavior and attitude when you announced your engagement to us. We've been terribly sad not seeing you and being part of your lives, and feel terribly disappointed with ourselves for the way we acted toward you, Andre, and awful about not giving you the unconditional love you deserve as much as our Dawn deserves it. We hope you can understand, Andre, that we grew up in immigrant homes and were taught racism and bigotry toward outsiders. We never really thought about our attitudes and how wrong they were until the last two years. We apologize for that.*
>
> *We've actually gone to a therapist for professional advice, which you know is not something we ever supported or would have considered in the past. We hope you can put aside your anger, pain, and hurt, and accept our eagerness to build a relationship with your family and to show you both that you are and will always be a part of our family.*
>
> LOVE,
MOM AND DAD

Do a "Needs Inventory" to Find Ways to Enhance Your Relationship with Your Family

A basic range of human needs must be met before a sustainable and satisfying relationship with your family can be established. When people make a contract to meet these human needs for and with each other, relationships tend to proceed smoothly and amicably. It's true that you can't negotiate such a contract with a person who is estranged from you, but if you succeed in opening the door—as Sylvia and Frank managed to do with Dawn and Andre—you'll have greater success in keeping that door open by remembering people's basic human needs.

You can safely assume that if you've had a breach with your family resulting in estrangement, you have not all been meeting each other's needs. Ask yourself if you can honestly say you have treated your alienated family members with respect. Ask yourself honestly if you remembered them on special occasions and had other ways of showing them you love them. Have you supported them and helped them feel empowered? Chances are, coming from a family that cuts off, you may find yourself needing to address the deficits in your repertoire of meeting the basic human needs of your family members.

The following list details basic human needs that are too often neglected, ignored, or downright violated in families that undergo a rift:

- To be respected
- To be remembered
- To be loved
- To be understood
- To be taken care of
- To be supported
- To feel empowered
- To feel accepted
- To be treated nonjudgmentally
- To be encouraged to feel self-worth and self-love
- To be treated with generosity
- To have our privacy respected and boundaries honored

This is the time to apply the process of taking an inventory of your relations with your family. Regretfully we can't necessarily expect that our family members will reciprocate and meet our needs; once again, we have no control over anyone else's behavior but our own. However, we can be grateful that we have the strength, hope, and wisdom to lead by example. Often by changing how we treat other people, they change how they respond to us. We can hope that our families will welcome our efforts and will respond to our new behavior through the inspiration of the examples we set.

Be Creative in Planning Shared Experiences to Bolster a Newly Defined Relationship

One of the reasons dysfunctional families continually and repeatedly get into trouble with each other is the family's history of ineptitude at knowing how to build positive experiences—experiences that can redefine and recast family conflicts. Very often families limit their contact to holidays and life-cycle celebrations, occasions that are often stressful and anxiety provoking. We are all familiar with the paradox that such allegedly loving and festive occasions as Christmas or the Jewish High Holy Days are so often tainted by memories of family feuds, but in troubled families, this is almost always the case. The same holds true, of course, for birthdays, anniversaries, and life-cycle events such as births, marriages, and deaths.

All the above occasions are anticipated with great hope and reinforced by Hallmark card images with which few families can compete. Disappointment and hurt then ensue, sometimes fueled by alcohol, and more negativity and dysfunction accrues in the family's history.

Fran and George are a middle-aged couple who came to see me because of conflict between their grown children. George began the session telling me that "when our twenty-six-year-old son told us he was gay, we weren't exactly shocked nor were we especially upset. Gary has always been atypical and unique, and my wife and I have always adored him and accepted him, as we have all three of our children, for who they are. My oldest son, Rick, is very similar to me. He grew up loving science, excelled in academics, and like me, has gone into medicine.

"Gary was always artistic, and never particularly liked school. Nonetheless we expected his gifts as an artist and illustrator would lead him to a solid career. And we were right. He's doing great as a freelance illustrator, making enough money to support himself and to spend time pursuing his first love, painting. When he told us he was living with another man as a partner, we were fine with it, as was his brother Rick. Our daughter Randy, however, had a very different and very upsetting, unsettling response."

Fran then picked up the story: "Randy is our youngest child and the only girl, and now in her senior year of college. Gary, our middle child, was always close to both his brother and sister, and when Randy responded, two years ago, to Gary's coming out with an outburst of negativity, Gary was terribly upset, as we all were. George and I talked with her repeatedly about her judgmentalism and intolerance, and we privately hoped it was just immaturity and her own struggles as a college student without a clear direction that led her to be so nasty to Gary.

"She's slowly developed a distant acceptance of Gary for who he is, and they've had polite but reserved contact over the phone and via e-mail for the last year. However, for two years now they've avoided being in the same room together. It's weird for us, and upsetting, and we're at our wits' end in trying to find a way to normalize our family again.

"When Gary and his partner Troy celebrate a holiday or occasion with us, Randy always finds a way to bow out and avoid the occasion. She's maneuvered to exclude Gary from any opportunity to meet her boyfriend, and now she's telling us that they're going to be engaged, she thinks, by the time she graduates college this spring. In the meantime, Rick's wedding is coming up next October, and we're terrified to let the current rift fester and risk an uncomfortable scene at his wedding. We've got to resolve their rupture, we feel, before it gets more out of hand, and we feel it will if one of them maneuvers to avoid their brother's wedding."

When I explored with George and Fran how they'd handled the split between their kids, I suggested to them that they had been, perhaps, too laissez-faire about the situation, and needed to try to be more demanding and insistent that the family reach a solution. They hadn't liked Randy's demands, subtle and covert as they were, to honor her wish to stay away from Gary and Troy, but they capitulated to her wish, feeling they were doing the right thing. The same held true for Gary's insistence that Troy, as his partner, had to be accepted by Randy, and that he wouldn't get together with her without Troy being present. Fran and George had accepted this proposition in the same loving but, in my opinion, misguided respect for each of their children's autonomy.

"You're entitled to make demands on your children, even if they're adults, just as they've made demands on you," I said. "I would insist that Gary and Randy meet at your home and have dinner together with you, with their brother Rick present, too. I would ask them to do it as a gift to you, as a way of showing you they love you. I think that's fair of you to ask as parents, given how you've supported each of your children and demonstrated your love over the years.

"Mother's Day is coming up next month and Father's Day follows shortly after that. Tell Randy and Gary you want this family dinner as a gift to celebrate both of these holidays. Make it clear it's the only gift you want from them. If necessary, tell them that if they love you, they'll agree to it."

George and Fran reported at their next visit that their children had reluctantly and somewhat resentfully agreed to the dinner, and asked me how to ensure it would be a success. While I told them I had no guarantees, I suggested they try to keep the conversation away from the ongoing feud, and instead try to jolt each of them into remembering that they once had a loving and accepting relationship. "Find ways to remind them of what they once appreciated and valued in each other, and try to create overall an evening that might lead them to reconnect and want to rebuild."

Fran and George were delighted at the outcome of their Mother's Day and Father's Day dinner. "After some initial discomfort," George said, "I told the kids that I had recently found this great video of when they were kids. It was actually a video that Fran and I love to watch. We knew none of our children had seen it in years. It was taken over the course of the summer the year after I bought our first video camera, and the children were five, nine, and eleven years old.

"Randy actually didn't quite remember that summer, as she was very young, but we had gone to visit the boys at camp, and the video shows how excited they were to see their sister, and we had these great shots of Gary taking his little sister by the hand, and her beaming at how he showed her around. Later on in the video there's shots of a family trip we took to Colonial Williamsburg at the end of the summer, and there's this great footage of all three kids when we had let them rent period costumes for the day and they were running around laughing hysterically at how funny they all looked."

Fran continued: "Then we ate. I made my meatloaf and mashed potatoes, which was a favorite dinner for all the kids when they were younger. The video had put everyone in a great mood to reminisce, and by the time I surprised everyone with my chocolate layer cake that I had always made for each of their birthdays, I somehow knew it would be OK again between Randy and Gary.

"I couldn't help crying when at the end of the evening Randy said she was sorry she hadn't met Troy yet, and asked Gary if he'd be willing to get together with her and her boyfriend for dinner. When Gary put his arms around her and hugged her and said of course he'd be delighted, I looked over at George and he also had tears in his eyes."

While not all attempts at reconciliation work out as smoothly and happily as this family's did, the principle of attempting to build on past experiences and create new shared, happy ones will often eventually change the hue of a family relationship. Active steps in orchestrating the event apart from the stress of a holiday, birthday, anniversary, or other life-cycle event always makes the initial reunions go more smoothly. Instinctively, Fran and George knew they couldn't allow their family situation to fester and risk an accidental flare-up of the feud at an event such as their oldest son's wedding.

From how this couple handled their problem, we can also see the principle of building on positives. Without active leadership and careful planning, it's all too easy for family members to slip back into negative postures with each other. Their needs must be acknowledged and steps be planned to meet them either by an explicit contract to avoid discussion of irreconcilable difference, or by a strong leader who will quickly veto any regressive and destructive behaviors on anyone's part.

"No More Dredging"

One family I know that has recovered from a devastating estrangement has adopted the motto "No more dredging," which they use to remind each other to stay away from volatile issues from the past. Another person I know who has mended a family rift tells me he continually reminds himself, as well as his sister and mother who tend to be belligerent and negative, "No negatives. We don't want a repeat of any of the bad stuff we've inflicted on each other before, so we'll follow the No Negatives rule." He told me, "I get tired and resentful saying it sometimes, but it works, and it's much less tiring and upsetting than the total cutoff we dealt with in the past."

Another important issue in ensuring positive experiences with a volatile family is to make sure boundaries are respected and to plan visits and experiences that are not encumbered with too much physical proximity or too much concentrated time together. One couple I worked with used to visit the wife's aging parents in Florida for one week a year. Inevitably, the trip would be disastrous. They would all become edgy and irritable after three days, and it would inevitably escalate into a major war by the end of the week.

"It would be just too long a stay, and we'd all feel trapped," the wife told me. "Finally, three years ago, the fighting escalated to a regrettable level, and we stormed out of my parents' home both giving and receiving threats that we'd never speak again. Upset as I was, it was actually nice to not speak to them for a few months, but then my mother's birthday was coming up, and I just felt I'd regret escalating this feud even more by ignoring her birthday."

They've learned to help prevent such estrangements by shortening their visits to a weekend at a time. "We also decided, despite my parents' initially strong objections, that we'd take a room at a motel near their house. The ability to have our privacy at night and to wake up without being bombarded by my mother's chatter leaves me in a much better mood.

"My parents won't admit it, but they also are in a better mood, and despite their protests about the shortness of our stay, seem to have had enough of us after a few days, just as we have had enough of them. This new way of seeing them has allowed us to actually leave there recently with relatively pleasant memories, and we've actually enjoyed our time with my parents. That pleases me, as they seem to be rapidly aging, and I know at least now that I won't have terrible regrets should something happen to them."

Bucking Tradition

It generally takes some effort to see what steps you need to take to create positive experiences when you attempt to reconcile with a family that is easily provoked into estrangement. Families have traditions in the ways they connect with each other, and it's not always easy to define which aspect of the tradition *must* be changed in order to ensure harmony and build positive experience.

One of my clients, Alex, went to visit his family in California every year. His parents had retired and were living in a golfing retirement community. Alex and his wife usually had a miserable time and felt frustrated due to his family having a tradition of guests not renting cars. "They insist that whoever comes to visit them shouldn't 'waste' their money on a car rental. I know my sister and her husband put up with it, as do my uncle and aunt when they visit. I don't know if it bothers any of them like it bothers us, but my parents' game is to say we can use their car whenever we like—which never happens. Yes, I can use the car and drive it, but my parents then always find a reason that they have to be part of the plan, and I then feel trapped over and over again."

I asked my client why he didn't just rent a car. He was a grown man, and he and his wife rented cars whenever they'd go anywhere else. He looked at me dumbfounded and said he'd never thought of doing so. He said his parents would always get his flight information and tell him they'd be at the airport. "I just never thought of rocking the boat. It's the way we've always done it, and it didn't occur to me that I could do it differently. Sure, my parents won't like it, and they'll tell me I'm wasting money and that I'm a spendthrift, but hey—what are they going to do? Tell us we can't visit them if we have our own car? I doubt it."

Before his next visit, he didn't discuss it in advance with his parents, but reserved a rental car when he made his flight arrangements. "When they asked what time they should be at the airport to pick us up, I told them it wouldn't be necessary, that I'd rented a car and would be driving directly to their house. They were actually dumbfounded and didn't know what to say, so I used the opportunity to get off the phone. 'I have to run into a meeting right now,' I said, 'but I can't wait to see you tomorrow. Bye.' This trip went much better, and I actually think my parents felt unburdened rather than resentful by my renting the car. I still don't understand, though, why I was blind to this option until you suggested it."

"Old habits die hard," I said, "and traditions don't change without careful strategizing and looking at all your options."

The Science and Art of Family Negotiations

Ultimately, in families that are able to negotiate a mutual meeting of each other's needs, it becomes easier to build shared positive experiences. In the science and art of negotiating deals, the best and most successful negotiations leave both parties unhappy about some things but happy enough about other aspects of the negotiation to be glad of the deal. That makes for a situation where both parties feel that on balance they can accept the terms and be relatively happy with them. Families that negotiate healing estrangements in this manner will have more success in building positive shared experiences than families that cannot arrive at satisfactory negotiated terms of connection.

For example, Roy and his family, following an estrangement, were able to negotiate a deal that they could all live with. Of course this wasn't negotiated as smoothly as a business negotiation. There were lots of baby steps for both Roy and his parents to reach an agreement, and some very painful concessions before they arrived at a place where they all felt respected and able to sustain a relationship.

Roy, a young actor I work with in therapy, grew up in the South and was worried about how his parents would respond to him as a gay man, given that they were devout Christian fundamentalists. He discovered that his worry was merited; his coming out to them began months of painful estrangement. Roy finally decided to e-mail his parents and try to be clear about his needs and ask them to give him greater clarity about their needs. He also made it clear that while he was not happy with the estrangement, there was no way he could or would or wanted to change his sexual orientation to heal the rift.

He explained that he needed his parents to accept him as a gay man, to include his life partner, Richard, in invitations to family gatherings, and to stop sending him religious information about the evils of homosexuality, and stories about how God helped homosexuals realize their errors and enabled them to have a "normal" life. "Fortunately for me, they went to their pastor, who, despite being a born-again devout Christian, has some basic sense and respect for diversity. It was also helpful to them that he told them about his own struggles in accepting his daughter's choice to marry a man of the Jewish faith and convert to his religion. His telling them that he felt God wanted him to accept his daughter's choice even if he wasn't happy about it, and that God wanted them to accept their son's choice even if they weren't happy about it, helped them to get closer to accepting me.

"On their side, they slowly explained to me their needs. They needed me, they explained in a series of painful e-mails, to include them more fully in my life and stay in touch with fairly frequent phone calls and e-mails. They also said they wanted at least some 'alone' time with me when we visited each other. I didn't really like this, but I could live with it and liked it better than the estrangement."

Slowly and painfully, Roy and his parents learned to abide by each other's wishes and began spending time on the phone for the first time since he had come out to them. Roy still wished his parents could be more positive and supportive of his choices, but felt he could tolerate their feelings if they didn't criticize him or bombard him with religious literature. When they all felt comfortable enough about this less-than-ideal family situation—Roy wishing his family were more positive and supportive but grateful that they learned to respect him, and his parents wishing their son would marry and have children but pleased that he would include them in his life—they were able to plan an in-person visit.

"The funny thing about our first visit to them was that we were all tremendously anxious and uncomfortable, but much to my parents' surprise, they both couldn't help really liking Richard, my boyfriend. Unlike me, Richard is a sports fanatic, especially baseball, which is my father's greatest love. They were able to talk baseball for hours, much to my dad's amazement. At the same time, Richard's a chef, and my mom felt both completely flattered by his appreciation of her cooking skills, but also grateful when he showed her some of the tricks of the trade when she was preparing dinner. They can't quite bring themselves to say that they like Richard, but their attitude shows it and that's good enough for now."

The successful family mendings we've seen in this chapter have occurred because someone has been willing to be in the driver's seat and assume responsibility and initiative for changing the way the family members behave toward each other. They've also been successful because the family has been responsive and able to make the necessary acceptance to move into more positive mutual agreement.

When Alcohol Is in the Mix

Over the years in my work with clients, I've encountered a host of examples of ways in which people can better and differently manage families that are able to accept their invitation to forgive and forget and move on in a new way. A number of people I work with have identified alcohol as the element that has always fueled family feuds in their families. Sometimes this problem has been managed by maneuvering to have contact with family members only in situations where alcohol is not served.

"We used to see my family about six times a year for dinner, and dinner always began with a more-than-ample cocktail hour. That's how it is with my family. Invariably the drunken joviality, which I'll admit I enjoy, leads to arguments and at times has led to embarrassing public scenes where dinner has been cut short with someone storming out shouting, 'This is the last time you'll ever see me. I'm done with you.'

"The last time my father did that to me, the estrangement lasted two years, and it was awful. When I finally felt ready to reconnect, he and my mother were amenable, but I made it conditional that we all do gatherings that don't involve drinking. Basically, that's meant meeting for lunch or brunch two or three times a year, since my parents aren't willing to forego cocktail hour and wine with dinner. It's not a great situation and certainly doesn't make us feel terribly close and connected, but it feels better than the total estrangement I had felt."

Another client I work with told me about a history of intermittent estrangement with his heavy-drinking sister and brother-in-law, as well as his heavy-drinking son and daughter-in-law. "What I realized was that I was equally culpable in the fights. I like to drink too, and drinking loosens me up like it does them, and I find that either I respond in an overreactive, destructive way to their provocativeness, or that I myself act provocatively and give them grounds to be furious.

"I've learned in recent years that if I don't drink around my family, I'm able to stay in control—stay out of the line of fire, so to speak. I'm also able to contain any impulses to tell any of them exactly what I think of them. That always leads to trouble, often to lengthy estrangements. I realized I'm not an alcoholic. I'm fine when I have drinks with anyone else, but with my own family, I have to remain sober. I guess you could say I'm a 'family-specific alcoholic,' if there is such a thing."

Family Strategizing: My Experience

When Cindy and I managed to open the door to healing the rift with my family in 1991, we each made a personal inventory about our contributions to the family problems. We also took specific actions similar to the ones I've suggested to you in this chapter based on my clients' experience. One aspect of our management of my family was particularly helpful: to be hyper-vigilant regarding my family members' birthdays and anniversaries and to be especially connected when either of my parents was sick.

Showing them this concern made them feel loved and helped ward off my father's habit of enumerating my life-long acts of injustice toward him and the rest of my family. We also decided to never bring up either my parents' or sister's forgetfulness regarding our own anniversary or birthdays, as well as never mentioning their neglect, at least as we perceived it, for our family's illnesses and crises. This was a major way in which we applied the principle of "what you see is what you get."

We also carefully strategized our get-togethers so they would work for all of us. One year we gave my parents a family trip with us to Las Vegas for a weekend. This was exceptionally successful in building accruals of positive experiences. We didn't choose Las Vegas because any of us has a special interest in gambling. We picked that location because it allowed for each of us to happily pursue activities we enjoyed. My parents played golf, Cindy and I worked out in the gym and sat by the pool, and Steven and Kenny happily amused themselves in the various theme parks available to them. Going to great restaurants was one of the few interests we all shared, and Las Vegas allowed for us to go to three different terrific restaurants without the usual stressor of either my parents or us having to contend with the normal traffic nightmares of going back and forth between our homes.

We managed together for a decade in this way, with only minor eruptions of hostility and occasional fights, but none getting out of hand to the point of estrangement. Unfortunately, life events and individual changes within family members didn't allow for the mended and carefully managed family contact to continue. For many of you, mending the rift in an enduring way may also not be possible. We'll look at how to come to terms with that possibility as we move into the remaining chapters of this book.

8

Build Your Second-Chance Family

We usually think of family as a unit made up of parents and children linked to grandparents, aunts, uncles, cousins, and other blood relatives with a shared ancestry. This family tree, of course, continually receives additions through marriage, and a well-functioning family will not only be able to adapt to these additions, but generally go out of its way to welcome them.

However, there's another definition of family, one that broadens its meaning and scope: a family can also be a group of people connected through fellowship. *Fellowship* suggests a voluntary coming-together, joining through the desire to join, choosing to ally oneself with other people with whom one feels a special connection. It is from this broader definition of family that we derive the concept of the second-chance family. In a second-chance family, members cultivate friendship, solidarity, and camaraderie because they want to cultivate it. It is an especially crucial and healing notion of family to victims of family rifts, for whom a second-chance family can take the place of blood relationships that may, temporarily or forever, simply not be able to provide the security and love they need and deserve.

It's enormously painful to acknowledge the powerlessness that family estrangement makes you feel, and to work out ways to move beyond it. As we've seen throughout this book, when you do finally acknowledge it, one of the best tools for moving past the bad feelings is to focus on the ways you *are* powerful. You may not have succeeded in getting the love, respect, and companionship you wanted from the family you started out with, but you do have the power to get love, respect, companionship, warmth, and friendship from the families you create in your life now. In other words, you can choose a new and more loving second-chance family any time you want.

As you know from my own story, it was difficult for me to acknowledge my powerlessness in my biological family, despite clear evidence that, however hard I tried, I could never wrest what I needed from them. It was only when I could fully acknowledge that my family wasn't equipped to meet my needs— that, as the saying goes, I couldn't get milk at the hardware store—that I could change my focus, and seek out and create a nurturing family of my own.

This second-chance family—my wife, my children, those of our blood relatives who choose to remain in our lives, and our closest friends who are like aunts and uncles to our children and like brothers and sisters to my wife and me—do respond to me as a husband, father, friend, brother, and human being in ways that I have learned I have the right to expect. In fact, I realize that the only impediment to achieving the closeness and love from a family that I've experienced in my second-chance family was my former assumption that I couldn't have such a thing. I had to change that assumption—change my attitude toward myself—before I could awaken to the second-family opportunities, which I now know are abundant. A part of what has enabled this change is hard to define, but it's turned out to be essential. It's what I call the spiritual component.

Spiritual Healing

Until now, we've mainly focused on family estrangement from a psychological perspective, investigating ideas and tools crafted by psychological wisdom and experience. But now I'd like to expand our tool kit to include something perhaps less tangible but no less powerful—in fact it's the most powerful tool we can make use of: the spiritual aspects of healing. Nine months into my family estrangement in 2001, I was challenged to call upon all the spiritual resources I could muster up to get through the painful and demanding days, weeks, and months that began with the September 11 terrorist attacks on New York City. It was during this time of agony that I learned just how important the spiritual is to healing of any kind.

On the morning of September 11, 2001, I had an 8:30 A.M. session with a patient who is a playwright and screenwriter. She told me that the screenplay she was writing involved a Jewish man whose brother dies suddenly and unexpectedly. She asked me to explain Jewish customs surrounding death and mourning, and in particular asked me what the Kaddish, the Jewish prayer of mourning, was all about.

I explained to her that the theme of Kaddish actually is not death but rather the greatness of God. As a secular Jew, I found meaning in the prayer because of the sense it gave me of connection not only to the larger family of Jews that has existed uninterrupted for millennia, but to the family of man. The Kaddish also serves as a reminder that while loss caused by the death of a loved one may feel so devastating as to make the mourner feel like he or she can't go on, it is our duty to go on—to honor the person we have lost by recommitting ourselves to life. I told her I also thought of the Kaddish as a prayer for peace, both within myself, and peace in, with, and for the extended family of humanity.

At about 9:20 that morning, just as she was leaving my office, my patient asked me to recite the Kaddish so that she could get a feel for it as she went on with her writing. Having grown up going to synagogue weekly, I had heard the Kaddish recited thousands of times, and repeated it for her now. My patient thanked me and left my office. I had no idea that at the moment I recited the Kaddish my best friend Tom was either dead or struggling to survive in a towering inferno. I had no way of knowing that life, as I and all Americans had always known it, had changed forever.

In the weeks that followed, I often thought of this moment of reciting Kaddish—not knowing how completely appropriate its emergence then had been. I often repeated it to myself. It soothed me, helped me to keep going, helped me to stay strong for my wife and children, for my patients—and, in some basic way, just seemed like the right thing to do. I'm sometimes still overwhelmed by the synchronicity of these words having been the last I uttered—right before entering the maelstrom of the events of 9/11 and their aftermath.

Part of that maelstrom involved responding to a call I heard on the local news for trained mental health volunteers to go to the Red Cross to work with victims of the tragedy. (Mayor Giuliani had just set up a mental health hotline for the families of victims who needed immediate attention.) I spent that night—perhaps the longest night of my life—talking to people who were missing relatives and still hoping against hope that they had survived the attack. At the same time, I was praying that my friend Tom would be among the survivors. At this point no one had any idea of just how few survivors there would be.

That night it was clear that my skills as a psychotherapist were all but useless. The only tools I could draw upon were human ones. "My prayers are with you," I said to my callers. "May God bless you," was their reply. I treated everyone I spoke to with as much kindness and love as I could summon up. As the days went on, kindness was epidemic in the city. We had to stick together and love each other; we knew it was the only way to survive. I and many other New Yorkers turned to our most spiritual selves as we mourned as a community, as a family.

But as I struggled to recover from these losses, and immersed myself in volunteer work, it became more and more clear that kindness and compassion, community and friendship, unity and team play were the only ways to recover from *any* tragedy in life. It became more and more clear to me that the answer to coping with a family estrangement lay much more in the realm of spirituality than in psychology. The lessons of 9/11 applied as forcibly to family rifts as they applied and still apply to healing the global divisiveness all of us face today.

My Own Second-Chance Family

On September 11, my friend Tom was working in his office on the 104th floor of one of the World Trade Center towers, minding his own (and his company's) business, when he was snatched from this world by the evil explosion of terrorism. Tom's death meant more to me than I can describe. We were like brothers. We shared an intimacy that went beyond friendship; it felt more like kinship and family. We loved and supported each other. We shared a bond in which we offered each other unconditional love, support, and trust. I had suffered the loss of close friends in the past, but Tom's death was much more devastating. I truly felt like my brother was gone.

Tom was an integral part of what I had come to think of as my second-chance family. Looking back at my life, I realized I had never felt a closeness or comfort with my family that ever went along with the concept of *family*; my own association with my family had always been riddled with anxiety, fear, worry, rage, and distrust. As a teenager, I had often adopted other families of close friends, preferring their company to that of my own family. In effect, although I didn't use the phrase then, I now realize I began creating my second-chance family as soon as I had the resources to spend time away from my house. Over the years the composition of my second-chance family has evolved and changed, but finding and connecting with others in a familial way turns out to have been my way of creating the positive and loving environment I needed and need.

Now, with Tom gone, there is a huge hole for me in that family, but I'm grateful to have the memories of Tom I do have—my friend and brother. Somehow these memories help to sustain me now, too, even after his death. Talking with my wife about Tom after his shocking departure from life, I spoke about how grateful I was that he at least had been able to come to my son Kenny's bar mitzvah. That Tom was there turned out to be much more important and meaningful to me than the sorrowful fact that my parents and sister and her family refused to attend. This was a stunning realization for me, and it went along with much of what I have ultimately learned in my process of recovery from 9/11 and Tom's death: not only that he'd been an important part of my second-chance family, but also that the loving power of that "family" really had become strong enough to sustain me—give me a sense of belonging that I'd never known with my family of origin.

Even more than that, I realized that the positives—the joys, pleasures, triumphs, shared experiences, warmth, generosity, love, and compassion of the second-chance family—could override the painful shortcomings of my family of origin. This had the force of revelation, especially because I had been struggling with this issue so painfully and profoundly for the entire preceding year. The impact of Tom's death contributed to my sudden understanding that the "new" family he had been part of had quite simply been saving my life. I had found the solution without quite realizing I had: that, with loving "family members" like Tom, I had created exactly the family I needed but never knew growing up.

The events surrounding the recovery effort from September 11, 2001, continued to help me understand this new concept—to clarify much of my thinking about recovery from family estrangement. Here I was going through perhaps the most profound and unsettling event of my life, and I found myself on the receiving end of an unending and limitless supply of support, love, caring, and compassion from people I'd chosen and who'd chosen me: what I now labeled my second-chance family. Although members of this family weren't always tied by blood, our interaction with each other could only be described as familial: I found myself being friend, brother, and caregiver to these people, as well as to the broader family of New Yorkers and Americans. This sense of chosen family is one in which we all can participate, and which those who've suffered from family rifts very much need to pursue and create in their own lives.

Finding Your Own Second-Chance Family: The Key to Healing from Family Cutoffs

Karl is a man who started seeing me for therapy for problems with his marriage as well as chronic depression and anxiety about never feeling well, despite the fact that he could find no medical reason for his various maladies. He didn't come in particularly to talk about his estranged family, and in fact had not even labeled his relationship with his biological family as one of estrangement, but over time he began to realize more and more how his history of having been rejected by his biological family had had a huge impact on his ability to enjoy life.

Karl began to accept that his physical problems, as his medical doctors had told him repeatedly, clearly amounted to hypochondria. His suffering was genuine, but his overinvolvement with the various maladies he felt were plaguing him was hurting both his career as an aspiring writer and his marriage. He could acknowledge that his obsessive medical research on the Internet and frantic and frequent doctor visits were making his life much more difficult than it needed to be, yet he felt powerless to stop it. His wife was beginning to be fed up with a husband who she felt was a "cripple by choice."

The eldest of three children, Karl had grown up in an alcoholic family. His brother Henry was one year younger than he and his sister Paula one year younger still. His father owned a thriving retail store in a Midwestern town and, despite his dad's chronic drinking, the family was economically comfortable. But they were comfortable in no other way. All three children felt frightened and intimidated by their dad's frequent drunken abusive rages. "My mom dealt with my dad, or actually avoided dealing with Dad, by being sick all the time. She virtually always got sick when dad got drunk—which was all the time. The more he drank and the crazier his outbursts became, the sicker she would become."

Karl said the pattern finally began to break up once the kids were all out of the house and his father had a heart attack which scared him into sobriety. "Without Dad's drinking episodes, Mom's hypochondria and need to dramatize what were pretty normal ailments seemed to disappear," Karl says, "and their relationship seemed to become friendlier. Of course the three of us were each so disgusted with our parents' treatment of us as kids that we had all gotten as far away from them as possible."

While Karl had never had a major fight with his family, nor were they officially estranged, for him "it was as if my family just ceased to exist." Karl drifted away from his sister and brother and their spouses and families as well. "It was like there'd never been any bedrock for any of us. We just didn't really feel like family."

This amounted to a subtle but real family estrangement. Karl's parents moved to a retirement community in California, and Karl and his wife exchange Christmas cards with them but little else. None of it seemed like that big a deal. "My feeling is that my parents decided late in life in effect to be childless. They've just quietly cut themselves off from their grown children, as completely as they cut themselves off from us more abusively and dramatically when we were young. And while this doesn't make me feel great, I also don't think there's anything I can do about it."

When we began to talk about Karl's disconnection from his family and how similar his hypochondria was to his mother's, it became evident to both of us how much the symptom served to keep him connected to his family almost as a replacement for a real relationship. He began to recollect how as a little boy he was often sick; he remembered it as the only time he received attention, warmth, and caring from his mother, who was generally consumed with her own illnesses. The outcome of these behaviors was that Karl felt as lonely, bereft, and unsupported in his adult life as he had growing up.

Karl also told me that chief among his wife's dissatisfactions with him and their life together was his reluctance to get involved with a wider range of friends, and his resistance to socializing with the few friends they had made. Kris, Karl's wife, was a woman who had, in fact, also often been ill as a child, but unlike Karl took great pleasure in being healthy as an adult. She was unable to understand, respect, or tolerate Karl's hypochondria for much longer. He, on the other hand, complained vigorously about what he perceived to be his wife's frantic desire to go out all the time.

As Karl and I talked about these issues, it became clear to both of us that he had never really dealt with the pain and sadness of the estrangement from his family, and that the absence of an event or a fight had left a void that he had been filling with his increasing hypochondria. He also realized that he had fallen in love with Kris because of how gregarious and outgoing she was and how impressed he was by her intense relationship with her family and large group of close friends—an intensity and pleasure he, of course, had never known.

Karl called me one day between therapy sessions, sounding upset yet more alive than he usually seemed. He told me that he needed to change his next appointment with me because his wife's doctor had found a suspicious lump on her breast and was sending her for a biopsy. He wanted to accompany her to the biopsy, which was scheduled at the same time as his therapy appointment. Of course I readily rescheduled him.

When he came in for therapy that week, he talked about how scared and upset he was at the idea that there could be anything wrong with Kris. He also realized, he said, that his focusing on Kris caused him to forget about his ailments for the first time in months, and that since he had heard this news he hadn't thought about his physical health even once. He said he understood, not just intellectually but in his heart, that his ongoing complaints about his physical health were ways to ask for closeness with Kris, but somehow Kris's illness had jolted him into realizing there had to be better, more effective ways to do that.

This jolt awakened him in other ways. "I am just blown away by how wonderfully supportive Kris's friends have been to her. They're calling her continually to see how she's doing and asking if there's anything they can do for her. What's even more amazing is that I've gotten a couple of calls from the husbands of Kris's close friends, saying how this must be really hard for me and that if I need to talk about it, they'd be eager to sit down and talk with me.

"I feel like a real jerk now having accused her of frantic and obsessive socializing. I never realized how important loyal friends could be. How could I? I grew up with parents who had no friends, and I had no model for these kinds of supportive and caring relationships."

Happily, the lump in Kris's breast turned out to be benign; also happily, Karl was able to use the lessons he learned from this experience to change his outlook about his own life. He was also able to let go of his hypochondria. In effect Karl began to understand that he was already surrounded by a group of people willing to offer him the same love and support that they had offered Kris—a second-chance family. He realized that the only thing keeping him from taking advantage of this loving group of people was his own belief that it couldn't happen.

And yet, he says, "I guess I always had a clue that things could be different. Certainly that I wanted them to be. Again, I married Kris because she was healthy, and she knew what a close family was. I guess I wanted some of what she had but didn't know how to get it. Now I realize it was there for the taking and enjoying all along. Something just had to shift in me before I could see this. The prospect of losing Kris really did jolt me into a whole new understanding of how much I loved her—and now, how much I want love and connection in all of the rest of my life, too." This takes effort: Karl is bucking a lifetime of not having known what it was to be supported and loved, and he often feels awkward. "But I don't get sick anymore," he says. "So I guess I'm getting used to the idea that maybe I don't have to."

Lessons from "Minorities"

"You're talking about an idea, Mark, that members of the gay community have instinctively known for generations. So many gay people have been shunned by their families that it's always been natural to bond with our close friends in the community in a way that resembles family; for many of us, this family based on the commonality of being gay has been the only real family we've ever known. So I guess you could say 'second-chance families' isn't news to us."

Those were the words of my friend Jay Blotcher, writer and activist, as well as an integral part of my and Cindy's second-chance family. I then speculated aloud to Cindy that perhaps our affinity and bonding in familial "second-chance" ways had to do with feeling this commonality as well.

In fact, the more I thought about this kind of bonding, the more it appeared to me that many of our closest friends had histories of estrangement from their families or individual family members, usually based on their having chosen "different" or "unacceptable" lifestyles. Perhaps it was our mutual upset as well as the similarity of experience that caused us to bond in this way. I then began to look at others I knew who had strong second-chance family ties. One such person is a client of mine I'll call Yvonne. Yvonne was the daughter of an African-American father and a German-born mother. She had been conceived while her dad was stationed in Germany with the U.S. Army, and her parents hastily married before he was to be discharged so that they could easily move back to the U.S.

"Their marriage was short-lived," Yvonne explained. "I was the only thing they had in common after their infatuation with each other passed and they were trying to make a life together. I grew up with my German-born mother in Philadelphia, where my father's parents lived, and I saw my dad and eventually his second wife, my stepmother, on weekends. Mom took to drinking when I was young, and Dad's drinking steadily escalated, so it wasn't surprising that I coped with my loneliness and feelings of strangeness by starting to drink as a teenager.

"What I've come to realize over the years since I've been sober is that I never really fit in with either side of my family. My mom's family back in Germany hated me basically; they never really forgave my mother for getting married to an African-American, and at best they were civil to us both the few times we went back to Germany to see them. My dad's second wife is African-American, and her daughter from her first marriage is also, just as my two half-siblings are African-American. My dad's done the best he can, but he's always considered me the—well, white sheep, I guess. You certainly couldn't call me the black sheep if you looked around that family.

"So I really didn't feel I belonged anywhere, and while I still have a cordial relationship with my dad and his family, I don't consider them people I can count on because ultimately they consider me an outsider. Since my mom died I have no relationship with anyone in her family; they've made it clear they consider me a mistake, a black mistake, and they want no part of me.

"What I've seen over time is that my family—the people I count on, the people my daughter considers family, the people who count on me . . . well, either they're people from AA who've got similar family problems to mine, or like me, they're multiracial and don't feel they fit in with any racial group. It's funny. It doesn't really matter what racial groupings a multiracial person comes from; my husband's had an experience similar to mine with a Jewish mother and a Dominican father, and he too can't feel comfortable with either group. I think our quick comfort with each other had to do with our eagerness to establish a family of our own, and both of us coming to the marriage with families of choice as opposed to biological relatives as the family we introduced to each other."

Letting Others In: The First Step in Creating the Second-Chance Family

When I think back to the decade between 1991 and 2001 when I had a more amicable relationship with my family, particularly my father, I realize that during that time I was able to stop thinking about what a good father he was or wasn't, but rather focused on how good a son I could be. I accepted him for who he was and stopped taking his inventory. When I became angry, which is inevitable in any close relationship, I was able to say to myself "what I see is what I get," and decide on a new and different response to whatever was making me angry than I had chosen in the past. When I was upset that my parents had made plans with my sister and her family but excluded me and my family, I ignored my feelings about how terrible I felt they were being as parents, and instead focused on what I and my family could do to connect with them and create positive shared experiences rather than dwell on the negative.

The reason this relationship couldn't last, however, was that despite all the effort Cindy and I made to be a good son and daughter-in-law, my parents and sister didn't follow suit. They continued to focus not on how they could be better parents, sister, and in-laws to Cindy and me, but rather on the ways in which they felt we were still not measuring up. This intransigency spelled the demise of our shaky bond: a refusal to change focus.

However, herein lies a clue about what it takes for a second-chance family to form—something Karl learned when he realized that it was his own refusal to change focus that had kept him from enjoying the warmth and support Kris and her friends and family had always offered. Membership to any second-chance family is granted to people who focus on being the best "family members" they can be to each other. For me, this means focusing on being the best I can be to them. Seminal events such as Kenny's bar mitzvah and the terrorist attacks of September 11, 2001, again proved instructive in this regard, for they showed me just how loving, warm, and supportive the members of my second-chance family could be.

My real family—the family I had chosen and who had chosen me—were there for me on both occasions. They were there for me with solidarity, fellowship, companionship, support, presence, encouragement, comfort. Whatever I needed, whatever family support the situation required, I realized I could completely count on them.

At the same time, I saw the pleasure I could get in being the best family member I could be to my second-chance family, especially during the days following September 11, but also in various crises and catastrophes in recent years that have unfortunately befallen some of the people I love. The appreciation and gratitude I received in return, although not solicited, were very gratifying—a kind of reminder of how much I have appreciated similar behavior extended to me, an unconditional kindness and attention I had never known in my family of origin.

With regard to 9/11 especially, I also noticed that while I and many others initially reacted to the terrorist attack with a newfound patriotic zeal (sometimes bordering on xenophobia, racism, or an eruption of the desire to wreak revenge by attacking "them" back), these fanatical reactions began to diminish as the smoke slowly cleared. It occurred to me that the *family* war (waged by family members who cut each other off) is, on the other hand, sustained with an unrelenting ferocity much less amenable to the intervention of our civilized selves. It's as if the smoke *never* clears from that fire, no matter how long ago it was first set.

It has taken me many years to learn to treat my family with the same kind of "civilized" thinking that I now am able to bring to my assessment of our international dilemma. Overcoming our initial impulsive (if understandable) desire to "bomb the bastards" has allowed us to move on as a nation, to conserve our resources and focus on defending ourselves rather than contributing to further chaos and destruction. If only we could deal with the violence of family splits in similar ways.

The same need to moderate our impulses applies to learning how to keep from "bombing the bastards" in our families. For one thing, acting out vengefully and holding onto resentments amount to doing the same old thing in the same old way—which will produce the same old unprofitable results. Forgiveness with forgetfulness may indeed be idiotic, but allowing old sadistic patterns to remain in place opens us up just as much to new rounds of assault and aggravation. Nothing is healed. Everything is worsened.

Seeing Your Family of Origin Through New Eyes

The evolution in my thinking about the terrorist attacks to my home city encapsulates the evolution in my thinking about family life. All the years of high drama and acrimony were colored with hostility, bitterness, resentment, and anger—a toxic state I allowed my dysfunctional family to create within me. I realized over time that this unhappy, dark view of the world, this stance of being a victim and needing to fight, indeed reflected the worldview that I and many Americans allowed to grow within us in the weeks and months after the September 11 terrorist attacks.

Responding to having been physically attacked as a nation, many of us reacted reflexively to these attacks with the impulse to extract an eye-for-an-eye/tooth-for-a-tooth retribution. I and other people I knew had never before taken a political stance that was as bellicose and aggressive as we now brought to this tragedy. Yet, I eventually realized, this political stance was remarkably similar to the position I had been in with my family my entire life.

Over the course of recovery from family estrangement, I learned to focus my energy, attention, and emotional life on the family I created with Cindy and that we added to with friends and family members who wanted to be with us and whom we wanted as part of our extended clan rather than the family I'd started out from. This focus allowed me to feel less deprived as well as less angry. It even helped me reach a kinder and more benevolent stance toward my father, mother, and sister. The benefit of this has been that it's allowed me to proceed through life with less defensiveness and greater feelings of satisfaction.

Deborah, the dancer we met in Chapter 1 who was cut off by her family after marrying Jacques, an African-American member of her dance troupe, talked about a similar evolution within herself. "I've been going regularly to Al-Anon for some time now, and the people in the program have very much become a family for me. The friends Jacques and I have made together since we're married have also in many instances become like family. Some of these are biracial couples like ourselves, and some are white and some are black. In any case, I feel quite satisfied with my life, and I feel much more supported by Jacques, our family of friends, and my friends in the program than I ever felt earlier in my life when I was entangled with my alcoholic father and enabling mother.

"I've come a long way since this estrangement first occurred, and I've let go of many of my vengeful, spiteful, angry, and vindictive feelings and fantasies toward my family. I actually feel badly about my dad's alcoholism. I remember when I was younger, before his drinking was this out of control and when he wasn't such an angry and bigoted person, he could be a lot of fun and make me laugh and did things to make me feel special. He might have aged into such a great guy if he hadn't let his love affair with booze take precedence over his own well-being and that of his family. It's a shame that for whatever reason he couldn't do that.

"Instead of the chronic rage I felt for awhile about my mother not standing up to him and instead going along with his cutting me off, I've started to think about how oppressed she was by her own parents and what seemed to be their narrow-minded fundamentalist stance toward every pleasure in life. I can't say I was wild about my grandparents—all I remember is how shabbily they treated their daughter, my mother. It's no wonder she became such a dishrag and hasn't been able to stand up to my father."

This greater and welcome ability to understand and feel compassion for family members who have cut you off, once you start getting your needs met in a more gratifying second-chance family, happens to a lot of people. Often the new experience of love—of a kind of support you may never have known growing up—can have surprising healing benefits with regard to accepting aspects of your family-of-origin, to which you previously may only ever have been able to bring anger or despair. Another client of mine, Enrique, who recently talked to me about his feelings when his son was born, and how his joy about his child's birth overshadowed his estrangement from his family, illustrates this point:

"My family hated it when I married Marissa. They were really rude to her and her family and gave all kinds of reasons for their behavior, but ultimately I've come to the conclusion that it was envy for Marissa's family's wealth. I thought Marissa's family was really great to them and really tried to navigate a difficult situation with some kind of grace, but my family managed to find fault with whatever Marissa's family did or said.

"The fact that Marissa's dad offered me a job in the family firm at a great salary—well, rather than being happy for me that I got along great with her parents and that I was getting into a very lucrative and comfortable position, they felt belittled and devalued by her family's generosity—and envious that I would be more financially comfortable than they had been. Not that they were less than comfortable. My dad made a good salary as a civil engineer and they live a comfortable life, although for sure they're not as well-heeled as Marissa's family."

Whatever Enrique's parents' reasons may have been for turning their backs on their daughter-in-law and her parents, it just escalated into a worse and worse enmity. "When Marissa became pregnant with our son Adam, I thought for sure that my family would stop rebuffing the attempts at reconciliation that Marissa and I had repeatedly made. I was wrong. They seemed to be resolute about their stance that we'd committed some terrible crimes effectively meriting execution. Frankly I didn't know if my son would ever see his grandparents—or if they'd even want to see their grandson.

"I thought I was coming to some kind of acceptance of this," Enrique continued, "but I realized that I was just about always tense. I noticed that there was a joy and ease in other people I completely lacked. Over time I increasingly focused on the baby Marissa was carrying and became increasingly excited about the baby's arrival. But nothing could have prepared me for the unbounded joy I felt when Adam came out. When the doctor said, 'It's a boy,' I just thought: 'Oh my God. A son. *My* son. Not that I wouldn't have been just as blown away if it had been a girl. The miracle of having a *child*! It was like the heavens opened and the angels sang."

Despite the terrible rift that had grown between Enrique and his parents, he couldn't withstand the urge to call them and tell them they had a grandson. "Marissa's parents were already at the hospital and they were as elated as we were. I hoped so much that this birth would do the magic of reuniting me and my new family with my parents. So I called them from the hospital.

"My father answered, and I could hear him tell my mother the news. She got on the other line and very cordially they told me they were very happy for me. Cordially. No joy at all. I suppose it was some progress that they managed to be cordial. But instead of getting angry at them, I grew very, very sad. I realized in that moment how much they had cut themselves off from—not just from the joy of sharing happy events with Marissa, me, our new son, Marissa's family and our growing group of friends—but from the joy of just about everything.

"But then something strange happened. My mother asked me how Marissa was. Her voice had softened. She said she remembered what an ordeal giving birth can be. . . . "

Enrique's own voice softens as he recalls this moment. "Something had broken through to her. I felt like crying. Maybe they really were capable of letting us in—of allowing us to let them in. I told my mom that Marissa was fine, and that we'd both be a lot more fine if they'd come and see her and the baby. My father said, 'Well, of course we will. We wouldn't want to miss meeting our own grandson.'" Enrique was amazed—and had a whole new reason to feel joy.

Not that this has ushered in a perfect reunion—Enrique's parents are still full of wariness and mistrust. But a door has opened. Some channel of communication has been restored. The notion that even members of a family who had cut you off might see the light—or that you might, in the wake of experiencing love in your second-chance family, see the light and feel compassionate towards their blocks—is an important one. Change can happen. And again, one of its catalysts is something it's hard not to call "spiritual." Whatever moved Enrique and his mother and his father to open up to their lives a little bit more, it had something to do with a kind of spiritual surrender and acceptance.

Even the family of origin, or biological family, can become a family full of second chances. Sometimes, after an event like the birth of a grandchild, an opening presents itself, and family members may begin to explore new ways to relate to one another. Sometimes a tragedy such as the death of someone important to everyone in the family can induce this change. Whatever triggers this fortunate change, if family members want to and have the capacity to do so, they can reevaluate their stances on issues of autonomy and difference, even giving their own psychological make-ups a second chance. If motivated by love, they may find themselves able to accept a family member who they once felt had gone too far from the fold to be tolerated.

Circumstances in life can have a profound impact on people—even people once stuck in the seemingly intransigent enmity caused by family rifts.

But whatever the impact of circumstance, with determination and faith we can create family situations that serve us—if not with our families of origin, then with our second-chance families. All we need is the willingness to believe that we can find people to whom to give and from whom we can receive the love and support we deserve.

Here's a recap list of second-chance family attributes. These are traits to seek, to cultivate in the second-chance family you have the power to create for yourself—and that, in fact, you probably have already begun to create in your life.

Second-Chance Families
- Offer each other companionship, support, care, and understanding because they want to
- Give generously, willingly and spontaneously, not out of a sense of obligation or with the expectation of a payback
- Value trust and intimacy and strive to understand not judge
- Never resort to the Attila the Hun method of attack or the ostrich method of fleeing; they talk it through and work it out
- Don't dwell on what other family members could be doing to be "better;" they focus on what they could be doing to be better
- Attempt to infuse each other with joy, enthusiasm, and optimism, not gloom, anger, or depression
- Give you a second chance if you ask for one
- Replace vengeance with empathy
- Don't dramatize misdemeanors into felonies
- Embrace difference
- Respect choice

You'll find yourself feeling more gratification, serenity, and self-acceptance whether you use this list of attributes of the second-chance family as a guide to healing your family of origin or as a way to build the new family you've chosen. You'll find you want to delve deeper into the inner qualities that have made you feel better, and learn more about the traits of gratitude and generosity that you weren't fortunate enough to learn in your family of origin. The next step in your healing will help you more fully to integrate the qualities we've explored in this chapter.

9

Cultivate Gratitude and Emotional Generosity

No matter how much time passes or how far you've progressed in coming to terms with a family estrangement, the pain it has caused you will always be with you to one degree or another, waxing and waning according to life's circumstances and events. Mother's Day, Father's Day, Christmas, birthdays, anniversaries all will bring up difficult feelings about your family, whatever success you may or may not have had in healing the family rift. The task of weathering these hard times is always to recommit yourself to bolstering your own internal healing. You need to achieve and sustain some sort of peace within yourself about the crisis, no matter what new configurations a family's cutoff relationships may eventually assume, no matter what motives you're able to determine are or have been at the root of the conflict.

Sometimes new bridges can be built—a new capacity for loving, honest, and conscious contact can be achieved—between people who'd formerly dropped the guillotine on any possibility of communication, much less love. Sometimes the door can only be partially reopened, allowing a cooler truce; sometimes, because of inherently intransigent blocks (e.g., religious, sexual, or racial biases), the door must remain shut, at least for the foreseeable future. However, whatever the ultimate outcome of family members' behavior toward one another, your own private internal healing must come first. Without that, no family rift can be mended or reunion sustained—there can be no real, lasting peace in any family member's heart.

If you come from a dysfunctional family unloving enough to bury you for an alleged crime of having thought, lived, or expressed yourself in the "wrong" way, chances are good you've been brought up with an impoverished idea of emotional options. Choices in your emotional repertoire more than likely feel limited for a simple reason: you never learned from your family that there were many other options to deal with conflict. When all you learn from your upbringing are variations on fight or flight—that you've got only two choices, to be a people-pleaser or an injustice-collector—your sense of what's possible in life becomes strangled.

A family that cuts off will not likely have given you the experience of spontaneous expressions of unconditional love and caring. Hugs are given and received rarely, if ever. Expressions of appreciation, gratitude, warmth, and genuine interest, if they are at rare times part of the family's repertoire of behavior, will be clouded by their infrequency, the quickness of members withdrawing their affections, and the sense of obligation or payback they entail.

Fortunately, we have the capacity to integrate new emotional behaviors in our daily lives. It may necessitate, for some of us, devising and following a deliberate behavioral plan of action, consciously planned to avoid repetition of unprofitable behaviors we learned from our families of origin. I know this from my own experience as well as from my years of working with clients in psychotherapy. Any human relationship is like a plant. It needs to be tended, watered, fertilized, and cared for vigilantly. It will wither and die if it does not receive this attention.

If we come from dysfunctional families, we need to pay greater attention than most people do to learning how to become functional within the family. This takes work. Having learned to clam up when we disagreed with a family member for fear of being rejected, or to pretend to like or think certain things because we perceived that that was our only ticket to family acceptance, we usually don't realize that there is any other way to behave. Our second chance families require effort, too, but it's effort of a very different kind. We strive in those families to function in ways we *want* to function, ways that mirror our deepest desires and hopes—a quite different approach from the self-depriving one many of us grew up thinking we had to adopt.

I've conceptualized ten rules for keeping emotional connections working in ways that build positive accruals of shared family experience, and that will help you to overcome the deficits you may have experienced in learning healthy adaptive behaviors in your family. Adhering to these rules won't only help to keep your second-chance family functional, but will help you to feel better. That we have a right to feel better is, sadly, often surprising news to many of us who thought adapting to families always meant self-denial, not self-gratification.

These suggested rules are geared to freeing you from those kinds of negative assumptions about what success in a family entails. They are the building blocks of healing from family rifts. Their aim is to enhance self-esteem, improve our brain function, reduce depression, and cause us to feel more nourished and gratified: quite a contrast to the feelings of poor self-esteem, depression, and deprivation that we experienced with and from the kind of family that cuts off its members. These rules are also very much the converse of those adhered to by the injustice collector and the people pleaser. Following them will help to provide what is missing in anyone who comes from a family that cuts off.

Ten Rules for Cultivating and Maintaining Family Connection
1. *Assume responsibility.* Realize that it is up to you to create a strong family relationship between you and others in your family. This means not dwelling on what others may be doing or not doing to make it strong. Dwell on what *you* can do to make and keep it strong. Assuming responsibility for helping a family to thrive precludes adopting the kind of passive and reactive stance with which most people pleasers are familiar.
2. *Never tear a family member down.* No matter what you feel at any given moment about a family member, never humiliate, degrade, or cut him or her down. In other words, don't behave as you learned to behave in the family that cuts off; monitor your behavior and your responses closely to keep them constructive, not destructive.
3. *Accentuate the positive.* Positiveness is the glue that holds together the building blocks of a relationship. Not that this means whitewashing. Conflict and disagreement are inevitable in families. Handle these conflicts compassionately and in ways geared to demonstrating your willingness to understand the family member with whom you may have difficulty. Learn the language of connectedness, not alienation.
4. *Be patient when you communicate.* Understand that it may take many communications between and among family members to attain

clarity and understanding. If you step on a family member's toes, or if a family member, in the heat of the moment, says something to anger or upset you, treat it as a miscommunication—an invitation to find out more about why you are at cross-purposes. Try to see the other family member's side, and invite him or her to understand your own motives for your own responses.

5. *Don't turn a breach of trust into a resentment.* When family members let you down, or when they perceive that you have let them down, don't let this fester as a resentment. Embrace the idea that human beings are fallible and make mistakes. Turn any contretemps into an opportunity to find out more about whatever has caused the breach, and communicate your certainty that it can be bridged.

6. *Engage with family members creatively.* Don't fall into ruts of always treating or reacting in the same ways. Keep your family members' interests and desires in mind and surprise them every so often with an unexpected gift or by making plans that you know will engage them. Look for different approaches to connection than you may have tried. When you ask a family member "How are you?" give them the sense that you really want to know the answer.

7. *Don't employ avoidance as a tactic.* Be aware that avoidance is the enemy of sustaining relationships. Avoiding important issues and conflicts will ultimately drive you further and further apart from the people you love. Expressing yourself directly may occasionally cause temporary difficulties or passing ill-feeling, but it can also mark tremendous progress. If you are unhappy with a family member's behavior, communicate this—along with your certainty that whatever rift has occurred is temporary and can be healed.

8. *Build on your family members' strengths.* Whenever you find a nugget of something upbeat and positive in a family member's attitude, highlight and build on it. Reflect on the good and valuable aspects of your family members and share your happy evaluation with them.

9. *When a conflict is minor, keep it to yourself.* As important as it is to communicate with family members when you feel sufficient distress, it's also important to sit on it if the conflict is minor. Learn to keep your negative reactions to yourself until and unless you decide that

they're important enough to warrant discussion. Then do so in a way that is reparative and embracing rather than alienating and destructive.

10. *Rely on the healing aspects of time.* Remember that the sheer passage of time is your ally in building strong family relationships. What we feel in the heat of the moment is rarely what we'll feel after time passes. Understand that "this too shall pass." Having this kind of patience is part of the aim of all these rules: to make your family relationships a priority in a way that you never experienced in the family that cut you off. Allow yourself to take whatever time you need to register and empathize with your family members' feelings. Make that a priority over expressing your feelings—until you feel you've built a solid enough connection with your loved one to open the communication pathway between you.

The Importance of Empathy

We talked earlier about how the perpetrator of family estrangement is invariably an individual with an impaired sense of self: weak, fragile, and so deficient that he or she cannot perceive others' needs and feelings, much less respond to them in any positive way. This deficit signals a lack of empathy, which may be the most toxic aspect of dysfunctional family interaction.

What is empathy? Here's one definition I find powerful and useful:

Empathy is the capacity for and action of understanding, being aware of, being sensitive to, and vicariously experiencing the feelings, thoughts, and experience of another without necessarily communicating those feelings, thoughts, and experience in an explicit manner.

The key words here are *capacity* and *action.* You must have room for empathy in your mind and heart before you can feel, respond to, and act upon it. And the aim of empathy is action more than words. Empathy is something you demonstrate in how you treat people more than something to be explained. Not that words don't have a role in expressing empathy, but ultimately empathy is more profitably something you feel and do rather than simply say.

One of the most heart-wrenching stories I have heard over the years came from a client who grew up in a highly dysfunctional family with an alcoholic father and a narcissistic self-involved mother. When he was eleven years old, he said, he cut himself while playing in the yard. In his panic and fear, he rushed into the house. His mother shrieked, "You're bleeding all over my rug! Get into the bathroom now!" He then ineptly and fearfully tried to bandage himself as his mother focused on trying to get the blood stains out of her rug. This of course is an exaggerated example of a self-involved narcissistic mother who lacks empathy, yet it is a story of which we hear repeated (if not always quite so dramatic) versions in the childhood memories of many people who have suffered family rifts.

Adults who suffered a lack of empathy in their childhoods typically have a hard time believing that empathy is possible in their lives today. Fortunately, the capacity for empathy can be developed: empathy can be learned as a tool. Cognitive therapy can help in this regard. It requires overcoming the learned reflex usually felt by most people who have come from families who cut off. Learning to integrate a habit of empathy, of thinking of others first, and of putting ourselves mentally in the shoes of our loved ones, inevitably means the quality of our relationships will improve. This amounts to personalizing the admonition John F. Kennedy talked about in his 1961 Inaugural Address: "Ask not what your country can do for you, ask what you can do for your country."

Paul, another client of mine, was able to effect reconciliation with his family of origin through increasing his capacity for empathic connection. Paul's parents had cut him off three years ago when he married Diana, whom he had met when his work took him to a year-long position in London. At first, Paul's parents were charmed by Diana's English accent when they phoned him and Diana answered the phone. They were, however, not charmed to learn from Paul that Diana was not English. Paul explained that while she was brought up in England, she had been born in Jamaica, which was where her parents still lived.

"There was dead silence on the phone," Paul told me. "Then when I called them to tell them Diana and I were thinking of becoming engaged, they ganged up on me and stated their disapproval, and that if we got married they wouldn't attend the wedding. This not only made me angry, it fueled my determination to have the best, happiest wedding possible—which we did, in Jamaica, surrounded by Diana's family and all our friends. My parents, of course, boycotted the wedding, which hurt—but which I tried my best to accept philosophically. I wasn't going to let them ruin my happiness."

Three years later, Paul believes that he's learned and "grown up a lot. I've also learned from Diana how difficult it is to be 'different'—lessons she learned growing up in London and feeling stigmatized by belonging to a racial minority. Six months ago I got a phone call. I was shocked when I answered the phone and heard my mother's voice. I was even more stunned when she told me my dad had dropped dead of a heart attack the day before. Although I was completely taken aback to hear that my dad had died, my instinctual response was angry. I found myself blurting out, 'You don't think I'm going to his funeral, do you, after what he did to me? And even if I went, I wouldn't go without Diana.'"

My mom's response shocked me. "Paul, one of my first thoughts after I realized your father was gone was that I've got to reconcile with you and accept your wife and get to know her. I'm sorry, Paul. I was wrong. We were wrong. I wish your father, for your sake as well as his, had come to understand how wrong we were before he died. When I lost him, I realized how much I love my whole family and how insane it was to have cut you off, given how precious life is."

"Well," Paul continued, "for a moment I was speechless. All the anger and revenge I'd felt and wanted to act out against my parents sort of deflated. I guess, after all the work I've done on myself coming to peace with family estrangement, I had developed the capacity to be more kind. I surprised myself by being able to say to my mom—and mean it—that of course Diana and I would go to the funeral. She simply said, 'Thank you, Paul. That means a lot to me.'

"When I told Diana what had happened, she was as shocked as I had been. I asked her if she could forgive my mom and come to the funeral with me and, bizarre as it was, meet my family for the first time. She said of course she would if that's what I wanted.

"Actually," Paul said, "I'm not sure what caused me to change my position, but I think I did the right thing. I just don't quite know how or why it happened." I suggested that maybe, after having increased his capacity for empathy in other areas of his life during his marriage to Diana, that perhaps this enabled him finally to put himself in his mother's shoes, feel for her loss, and accept her apology. This may have helped him to get beyond his resentment, and agree to let bygones be bygones.

Paul said this made sense, and added, "I guess it's also because I had learned from Diana how difficult life can be when you're different from everyone around you. I knew my mom was pretty young to be a widow, and I knew she'd probably be the only widow among the group of friends they had built in the last thirty years. I feel for her. It's going to be hard for her. She'll be the different one in her group of friends.

"I don't know if my mom and I can ever have the closeness we had before all this strife and estrangement occurred, but I do know by now that my life gets better the more I learn how to be a generous person, and accepting her apology and request for a relationship can only make me happier, and make me feel better about me."

A friend of mine, Glenda, gives another good example of the benefits of learning to embrace empathy and the attitude of thinking of her loved ones over herself. "When I became engaged to Drew thirty-five years ago I was so happy until my family had to make me miserable. He had recently completed his degree in automotive engineering and his best job offers were all in Detroit. I come from Tampa and my whole family lives within fifteen minutes of each other. We had met at school in Atlanta, and my parents—and I—had always assumed I'd come back to Tampa and build a life there. Well, that would have been my preference at that point in my life, but anyone could figure out that there were no jobs for an automotive engineer in Tampa. And by that point, being with Drew was more important than being near my family.

"They made our engagement and wedding a misery with their negativity and ongoing campaign to change something that couldn't be changed: the fact that the only jobs in Drew's profession in those days were in Detroit. Well, over the years things never got better, and we became increasingly estranged, but that was compensated by the fact that Drew and I had three beautiful children and built a wonderful life together in Detroit.

"When Drew and I decided he should accept a job in Tokyo fifteen years ago, we felt it would be a wonderful experience for us and our kids, and it was. But my family considered this to be a move against them rather than a move for us and our kids. This really put the nail in the casket of estrangement. I tried to keep a relationship going with phone calls, letters, and repeated invitations to my parents to come and stay with us for awhile. Dad was retired, they were both healthy and traveled a great deal, but they wouldn't consider coming to see us. They wouldn't get over feeling that the whole point of our moving away was to get away from them.

"Then something very humbling happened to me. Our daughter Renee took a junior year abroad in Spain, met and fell in love with Xavier, who lives in Barcelona. She announced that they wanted to marry and would live in Barcelona. I was very upset—and underwent what I now realize were the same feelings my parents had about our living so far away from them. However, fortunately for all of us, I had learned a lot from my family's behavior thirty-five years ago.

"Suddenly I realized it was not so hard to put myself in Renee's shoes. She's in love and found a man who makes her happy, and she, like me, would follow him to the ends of the earth. The fact that Xavier runs a successful art auction house in Barcelona and that their prospects for a happy life there are so good has become something I've learned to feel joy about.

"I remember all too well how awful it was for me and Drew when my parents rained on our parade, so I'm forcing myself to be positive and keep my disappointed, angry, and hurt feelings to myself. Renee needs me to be happy for her, and I want to give that to her. I don't want her to feel the pain of rejection I felt from my mother, and I want to be happily involved in her life and have a good relationship with Xavier and his family. So I'm keeping my mouth shut, taking a refresher course in Spanish at Berlitz to brush up on the Spanish I learned in high school and college, and plan to become an expert at finding reasonably priced airfares from New York to Barcelona."

Glenda had not only allowed herself to be empathetic about her daughter's life choices. She also actively worked to find positive possibilities in a situation that at first seemed to her to be fraught with negatives and disappointment. "It's funny. I remember so little from my college Spanish class, but one word that's always stuck with me is *abuela*, which means 'grandmother.' I guess there's a reason for it, and now I know that the job I want to take on— once Renee and Xavier have the children they dearly want to have—is being the best long-distance *abuela* that anyone can be."

Remedial Education: Untwisting Twisted Thinking

In my personal quest to recover from having grown up in a dysfunctional family, as well as in my years as a therapist, I've learned that people who come from a family that cuts off need a kind of remedial education in how to have good relationships. People generally assume that emotional traits can't be learned, but in fact we can learn new repertoires of behavior, eradicating old behaviors that keep us locked in old emotional problems. As twelve-step groups say, you must act your way to new feelings—you can't feel your way to new actions. Learning to adopt new and healthier behaviors toward other people really can begin to change your emotional constitution.

One of the biggest wounds that requires remedial care is the feeling of being frozen (unable to react, to demonstrate caring, to defrost and allow warmth into our lives) that we often get from families where estrangement occurs. The behavior and way of thinking we learn in dysfunctional families can be called "twisted thinking." Fortunately, we can learn to think and act differently so that we're not sentenced to a lifetime of twisted thinking. Here are some examples of twisted thinking that characterize so many dysfunctional families:

- If you offer a child excessive praise, you will encourage a swelled head. If you tell children how wonderful they are, you will make them conceited.
- If you encourage a child to aspire to something greater, they will become "too big for their britches."
- If you tell any members of your family that you love them, they will take advantage of you.
- If you express excessive warmth to any family members, they will take you for granted.
- If any family members tell you they love you, they must want something from you.
- If you admit weakness or vulnerability, it will be used against you at a later time.
- If you help children with their homework, they will never learn to do it on their own.
- If your children do not want help with their homework, they are ungrateful.

What characterizes the opposite of this twisted thinking approach—what may be the most important remedial lesson you can learn to get out from under the weight of these crippling messages—can be summed up in one word: *generosity*.

Learning to Be Generous

"Paradoxically, it was the wife whom my daughter objected to so much who allowed me to reconcile with my daughter." Charles is a client in his seventies who had been cut off by his grown daughter, Jennifer, when he married Shirley a few years ago. "Shirley really tried to build a relationship with Jennifer when we were dating, but my daughter just wouldn't warm up to her. I actually wondered how Shirley could keep being so nice, given how unpleasant Jennifer was acting.

"The fall before we married, Shirley and I were making Thanksgiving dinner for both her son and his wife and children as well as my daughter and her husband and children. Jennifer and Jim never showed up—never even bothered to call to say they weren't showing up. Neither did they respond to any of the phone messages Shirley and I left that day, and they haven't responded to phone messages ever since.

"We were married without my daughter being present. She responded to the invitation with a short, sarcastic note, which was the only communication we've had until recently. My ex-wife, Jennifer's mother, hasn't been very happy about this. Ironically, she and I have a good relationship, and she told me that nothing she's said to Jennifer seems to make a difference. Jennifer won't tell her what she has against Shirley or why she won't have anything to do with her.

"Last month my ex-wife called and told me that our son-in-law Jim had a heart attack and was in the hospital. I was shocked; he's a young guy, at least relative to me, and I felt really badly for him as well as for Jennifer. Shirley told me I should leave a phone message for Jennifer, but, as concerned as I was, after all this time I didn't want to. She insisted on it—she's much more generous than I in that way.

"First I said, 'Why should I be hurt again when she doesn't call me back?' Shirley said, 'Because you're her father, and she needs her dad now. In fact, you should just go to the hospital and see Jim. I'll go with you. We should definitely do that.' 'Are you nuts?' I asked. 'No, I'm not nuts,' Shirley said.

'Jennifer would never make a scene if you came to the hospital. In fact, I think they'd both be overjoyed to see you and, in fact, to see us, and to have all this unpleasantness behind us.'"

Charles said he couldn't believe it, but Shirley turned out to be right. "Jennifer hugged me and began to cry, and cried in my arms saying, 'Daddy— I love you so much. Thank you for coming.' I started crying at that point, too. And then Jennifer said to Shirley, 'You're very kind. Thank you for being here, too.'

"Jim looked up from the bed, all wired to heart monitors and connected to an IV, and said, 'Well, I'm not happy that I had a heart attack, but if this is a sign of the benefits, it may be the best thing that ever happened to us.'"

Dora offers another story about the breakthrough emotional generosity can make possible. She told me she had no relationship with her parents or sister since she announced that she and her partner, Marian, decided not only to live together, but also to have a child together by Dora becoming artificially inseminated with donor sperm. "My difficulties with my family had long predated this bombshell. Even before Marian and I began living together, my parents couldn't accept my being gay, and continually denied it, telling me it was just a stage. When they saw I wasn't budging, they tried everything they could to get me to 'convert.'

"They did agree to meet Marian a couple of times in neutral locations like restaurants, but wouldn't invite her to their house and were icy towards her at best. But when Marian and I moved in together and announced our intention of having a child, they really went nuts and gave me an ultimatum to lose Marian or lose them. Well, I wouldn't be intimidated like that, and frankly I got much more love and support from Marian than I ever got from them, so my decision was basically a no-brainer.

"When our son Ruben was born, we were just so excited to have a beautiful baby boy! I guess I was still pretty naïve—I was very much missing having a family to share this with—so I called my parents to tell them. They said some very unpleasant things and hung up on me.

"Since then, I've really been looking at how other people were brought up and how other people bring up their children, and I've come to realize that I had a very distorted and deprived childhood. It wasn't that we were ever short on material possessions, but the cold and icy way of life I learned is something I just don't want for Ruben. I want to be sure I don't somehow pass on my parents' icy legacy to him. I know we tend to 'be our parents' without realizing it, and this has made me super-vigilant to be the kind of caring parent I never had."

Dora said that when baby gifts started coming in, she started to think about how gifts were handled in her family. "I realized that my mother had never wrapped a gift. On every birthday, I'd get clothes I needed and it would be given to me in the bag from the department store. Of course I had been taught to say I was happy and loved the gifts and to thank my parents, but looking back at it, I never got anything frivolous or fun, and nothing was ever presented in a festive and fun way.

"Then I started to think about the whole concept of fun, and how much difficulty I had loosening up and having fun. The only time I remember having fun with my family was occasionally at cocktail hour when both my parents would be in a great mood and joke around and lighten up, but that was rare and it always ended abruptly with some kind of fight.

"So, as Ruben's gotten older and I've been around more families with children, I've really tried to observe and learn how I can be a better parent. It's not that I ever neglect anything as far as Ruben's clothes or material needs or health. It's just that being warm, loving, and affectionate doesn't come naturally to me. It's natural for me to be reserved, distant, and detached, and I remember what a bad feeling that is for a child to have a parent who couldn't give hugs and say, 'I love you.' I never heard that as a child, and I don't remember anyone hugging in my family. Ever. So I've made an effort to emulate people I think are good parents in the ways I don't know how to be.

"I've also observed how Marian is much more generous than I am. She'll bring home a surprise for me at times—something useless, frivolous and generally absolutely adorable—something fun! Like one Halloween, she came home and shouted, 'Trick or treat!' She was holding a huge chocolate witch wrapped in orange ribbons in front of her face. Well, I just cracked up and kissed her and thanked her, but at the same time, I started to think, 'We both watch our weight, and we'll never eat more than a bite or two of that giant witch. What a waste of money!'

"It was like my mother's voice suddenly popped into my head. Luckily I was able to remind myself how much I cherish the spontaneous, fun side of Marian, so I kept my negative thoughts to myself. I realized that was a perfect example of the kind of thinking that I don't want Ruben to be plagued with. It's twisted and hurtful. I'm slowly getting to the point where spending money on something 'fun' doesn't strike me as wasteful."

The Power of Gratitude

Another client of mine, Bill, has been estranged from his family ever since he became sober fourteen years ago. One of the most powerful tools he has learned in his recovery from alcoholism is the power of gratitude, the ways that focusing on what makes you grateful can alter your negative assumptions and give you the strength to create and live a positive life. We've encountered this notion in Chapter 2, where I encouraged you to make a gratitude list and keep it with you to consult. Here we return to the notion—and the list. By now I can virtually guarantee it will have even more meaning to you than it did when we first investigated it. Here is how Bill learned its power:

"My life was really on the line," he told me. "I had a drug habit as well as drinking a dangerous amount of alcohol every day. I was having continual health problems and jumping from job to job, and thank the Lord I ended up in a detox ward rather than dead on the streets. I had blacked out and been found on the streets all beaten up, and when I woke up, I had no recollection of what had happened in the prior two weeks or even how I had gotten to the hospital. Thankfully, I had a terrific counselor in rehab who directed me to Alcoholics Anonymous and explained to me that I would probably die if I didn't stay clean and sober. I believed him. For the next year, I went to an AA meeting every day, and since then it's become my anchor in life

"My family didn't like me sober. They felt alienated when I wouldn't get involved in their drunken shenanigans. The yelling and screaming and fighting at holidays were dramatic and exciting, but quite intolerable if you weren't getting soused. I couldn't tolerate it once I was sober, and spent less and less time with my family on that account. Plus, they continually tried to get me to drink again. I mean it didn't even seem malevolent at times; they just felt I was too different and far away. It was like they missed the drunk. I didn't. I was scared. I didn't want to drink again. I had to withdraw from my family more and more.

"I tried to work it out with them, but it went from bad to worse. They kept criticizing me and making fun of my sobriety. Then I met Nora. She's great and she's sober, and we have a wonderful relationship. My family was horrible to her. They wouldn't come to our wedding because we decided we wanted a dry wedding. It was what we needed and made us happy. Our friends were fine with it and happy for us. Nora's family found it strange but they were supportive and they showed up. My family didn't. They raged at me and made fun of me.

"My mom called Nora and said we were embarrassing them, and how could they invite any of their friends or our relatives to a party without so much as a champagne toast? Nora was polite and told my mom she'd have to discuss it with me. I told my parents it wasn't negotiable. They didn't show up, and they basically ordered my brother and sister to not show up. That was it. I didn't call them after that. They didn't call me.

"It's been hard being estranged from my family, and it's been really hard to know how to be in a relationship with a loving person. I just don't have any experience to guide me. What I've had to acknowledge to myself is that my repertoire of instinctual emotional reactions is bizarre, inappropriate, and self-defeating. Growing up, I learned a range of emotion ranging from rage to paranoia to insensitivity to panic to fear. Not a great combination if you want to win any popularity contests or sustain a marriage," Bill laughs.

"I've found there's only one thing that I can count on to stop myself from indulging in my dysfunctional emotions and behaviors. That's gratitude. I've heard that from my sponsor since day one in program. However, it's still hard at times. That's when I actually use a gratitude list that I began when I was on an AA retreat years ago. It's the best medication for me.

"When I'm able to keep gratitude paramount in my thoughts—and that's not easy, as I grew up never seeing anyone express gratitude for anything, but rather complaints, misery, dissatisfaction, and envy in its place—but when it's paramount in my mind, it helps me control my impulses, say sweet and loving things to my wife rather than nasty argumentative things, it eliminates my paranoia and makes me feel less fearful."

Remember that gratitude is all of the following:

- Free
- Unlimited in supply
- Without harmful side effects
- Totally free of additives
- A plentiful natural resource that is always available when we seek it out

When I'm feeling overwhelmed and challenged by life, it's very important for me not to fall back into the discouraged and discouraging attitudes that I learned in my family. That's the important time for me to remember, like Bill, that gratitude is my best friend. The negativity and pessimism that we learned in families that later on cut us off can *always* be combated successfully with a strong dose of gratitude. Gratitude can accompany us on the uphill fights in life—a trait that I've found to be one of the best medicines for depression, self-pity, fear, and any other psychic pains we may have.

As a therapist, I've learned that gratitude is also my clients' best friend. In fact, it is an effective diagnostic tool: If a person can feel gratitude, he or she will definitely be able to get better. It certainly amounts to the best and possibly only treatment for self-pity. It can become a motivational speaker inside every one of us. When we feel gratitude and acknowledge our Higher Power's generosity, we are motivated to be the best we can be. When we are struck by personal tragedy, often the only way to get perspective on our troubles is by focusing on that for which we feel grateful. Without gratitude, people cannot love others, themselves, or life. It contributes to healing from family estrangement in incalculable ways.

However, it's often difficult to remember our best friend, gratitude, particularly when we feel trapped under a black cloud of despair and hopelessness—in particular, the black cloud of a family rift. We must not allow family members who cut each other off to relay their gloom and despondency to us as we progress in recovery. If you find solace and guidance in religious observance, certainly make this a part of your life—and use it as a forum to thank whomever you believe God to be for the undeniable resources you enjoy. However, for those of us who don't embrace the outlet of religion, it is essential that we find other ways to create reminders to draw upon gratitude. The benefits and rewards of doing this are great.

Bill talked about how he had learned to create and work with his own gratitude list. Many of us will also need to take these measures as we move on in our healing from family rifts—especially when we feel that old black cloud descend again. When my family estrangements first occurred, it was easy for me to fall into depression and self-pity, and like Bill, I turned at those times to my gratitude list. I think that all of us who grew up in families that cut off have deficits in our capacity for gratitude and need to increase that capacity—to remind ourselves to be grateful.

To that end, let's return to another more detailed version of the gratitude list I asked you to look over back in Chapter 2. Again, I can virtually guarantee that you will feel an even greater sense of thankfulness for the blessings on this list—and will be able to add more to it than you could think of when we started out.

Review the following list and check off what you can be grateful for. Write down your list. Keep it in your wallet or purse to take out when you feel depressed, frustrated, or angry. Add to your list daily. It's the best medicine I know to overcome the effects of a dysfunctional and unloving family.

Things I Am Grateful For
- My good health
- The good health of those I love
- My ability to overcome difficulties and struggle in life
- My strength
- My belief in a Higher Power
- My second-chance family
- My wife, children, friends, husband, brothers, sisters, and all those I love who offer me love in return
- My job and the fact that I can earn a living
- My relative financial comfort, especially when compared with most of the world
- My dog or cat or other pet
- My girlfriend or boyfriend
- My teachers, mentors, spiritual advisors
- My determination
- My ability to think clearly
- My ability to help myself
- My ability to express myself
- My capacity to give back to the world
- My innate intelligence
- My sex life
- My right of free speech
- Modern medical care
- Democracy
- The beauty I see when I look out my window

Learning to Appreciate

Expressing admiration and appreciation is another skill generally absent from our experience growing up in a family that cuts off. Appreciation is a close cousin of gratitude. In fact, the thesaurus considers them synonyms. However, I think they're distinct as qualities and abilities. While gratitude is a quality that can be reflected upon internally to make a person feel better, appreciation is an *expression* of gratitude toward another that will make both of you feel better.

Appreciation is also an ability that we may need some concrete help in learning to achieve. I recently talked to a client about this, Morgan, a man who came from a reserved, cold family with whom he hadn't had contact for years. He had come into therapy because of work and marital problems, but his history of family estrangement gave me many clues about his difficulties that he hadn't yet faced.

His wife's central complaint about him was his lack of demonstrativeness—physical and verbal—toward her and their children. "She says I'm never warm," said Morgan. "She says I'm just like my parents. I believe her because it's certainly the experience I had in my family and I kind of know how she feels. I'd like to learn how to express myself in a better way with her as well as with my kids. I don't want them growing up with the same lonely feelings I had growing up with my icy parents."

I suggested to Morgan that he didn't yet have the vocabulary for expressing warmth and appreciation, and that learning such a lexicon might help him. Talking generally about what he liked about his wife and children wasn't going to cut it. I knew his inability to be specific about his family's traits that he loved wasn't his fault. He didn't know any other way to be but emotionally shutdown and vague in his expression of appreciation.

I suggested that he try what I call an "appreciation exercise." The appreciation exercise is very simple; you can do it too. It's proven very helpful for people who come from backgrounds of family estrangement because, like Morgan, few of us know to employ a vocabulary of appreciation toward others, simply because no one ever taught it to us. Fortunately, learning to express appreciation is something you can learn to do with relative ease.

Pick a family member to whom you want to express appreciation. Then review the following list and check off each quality that applies to this person.

Ask this person if you may tell them what you appreciate about them. Explain, if you want, that doing so is part of your own recovery process in overcoming family estrangement. Keep the list handy. You may find you want to use it often. One guarantee: the person with whom you share it will be delighted.

Qualities I Appreciate About My Family Member

- Loyalty
- Friendliness
- Generosity
- Appreciation of others
- Appreciation of nature
- Competence
- Resourcefulness
- Artistry
- Thoughtfulness
- Perseverance
- Strength
- Experience
- Determination
- Sensuality and sexuality
- Fitness
- Good taste
- Expressiveness

- Warmth
- Kindliness
- Discretion
- Empathy
- Sensitivity
- Gentleness
- Compassion
- Intelligence
- Intuitiveness
- Humor
- Creativity
- Integrity
- Ambition
- Talent
- Flexibility
- Softness
- Curiosity

Use Your Dysfunctional Family as a Behavioral Guide

The above subhead may seem to contradict virtually everything I've said in this book about concentrating on the positive aspects of functional families and using them as your main guide. However, sometimes by reflecting on what the family members who have caused a rift haven't done, you can get important clues about what to do. In the words of my friend Marta, "When in doubt about how to behave—as a parent, as a wife, as a relative —I know if I do the opposite of what my parents and family did, I'll be doing the right thing. Seriously. It always works."

Marta, a retired opera singer who currently works as a vocal coach, has two grown children in their twenties, and her second husband has one son in college. "Complications abound when there are so many families blended together, but I must say, we all do really well. Ken and I each have worked out amicable and peaceful relationships with our ex-spouses, and all the children get along well enough, although they've never really lived together for any length of time and don't really experience each other as family. Ken and Peter, my ex-husband, actually really like each other. They've developed a nice friendship, which works great for my kids because Peter comfortably spends holidays with our family."

I asked Marta to give me an example of doing the opposite of what her parents would do, and to tell me why this worked.

"Oh, that's easy," she said. "Here's a good example. Max, Ken's son, is dating a girl neither of us can stomach. She's a spoiled kid from a rich family and for the life of me, I don't understand what Max sees in her, except I guess for the obvious: she is very pretty and has a great little figure. Maybe that's enough for a twenty-year-old. Ken doesn't particularly like her either, and she does something that I don't like, but it drives Ken absolutely insane.

"Max and Tara have been going out for about two years now, and every time we've taken them out to dinner—about eight or ten times so far—Tara will order the most expensive thing on the menu. Well, that wouldn't bother us if she ate it, but she doesn't touch it. I mean, she pretends to eat it—cuts it up, pushes it around her plate, takes miniscule bites. I don't think she's anorexic or anything. I think she just watches her weight carefully and probably feels she's had enough calories from the wine and appetizer. I can ignore it, but Ken feels that she does it to provoke him—that's it's some kind of weird spite work to waste his money."

Marta said she knew that her own parents would have gone absolutely crazy over this kind of behavior. "They simply couldn't have tolerated it and would have used it as a reason to make an ugly scene. I find myself wanting to suggest to Tara that she and I share a dinner to talk and get to know each other better—something I know my mother would have done, although with an ulterior motive—to turn the meeting into a scolding session. In fact, we did meet once for dinner on our own.

"True to form, although Tara said she was really hungry, she didn't touch a bite of her food. I very nearly reached across the table and strangled her. However, I controlled myself. Because I suddenly realized that this was the sort of thing my mother would never have let go. She would have whaled away at Tara for being so insensitive—it would have been the sole topic at the table. If my father were there, it would have been even worse. Loosened by a couple martinis, he really would have let the complaints and abuse fly. I can't tell you how often during my childhood we'd have ugly scenes in restaurants, with meals that became complete embarrassments, where we actually all walked out leaving our dinners untouched.

"But here's what really struck me. For whatever reasons, Ken's son Max loves this girl. And just as I was poised to attack her, I remembered this and held back. It was then it occurred to me—once again!—that one of the most valuable guides I had to how to behave was to reflect on what my mother and father might have done in the same circumstances. And then do the opposite."

My wife, Cindy, and I have learned to adopt a very similar philosophy. When someone in my second-chance family recently forgot my birthday—after Cindy and I had made a big deal of his birthday—we weren't very happy. When that kind of thing happened in my family, it invariably resulted in a crazy, raging phone call chastising us and telling us what awful children and relatives we were, and it went on and on until the fireworks were completely out of control. In this instance, Cindy and I thought about that, and we decided not to react. At a later date, when we were around this person and the subject of someone's birthday came up, I jokingly said to him, "I hope you'll do a better job remembering that birthday than you did mine." Enough time and distance had passed that I was able to say this in a jocular and sweet and nonthreatening manner.

This person was shocked and very upset with himself and apologized profusely, saying it would never happen again. I said it wasn't the biggest deal, but I'm still glad to hear that it wouldn't happen again. I felt very grateful that I had learned to do the opposite of what my family would have done. My reaction and later response were more generous and came from a wish to connect rather than to lash out. My wish to connect was heard, and the relationship gained from the encounter rather than deteriorated.

What Marta, Cindy, and I learned—and what I hope you'll learn—is that these kinds of positive connections and adaptive ways of resolving interpersonal conflict go a long way to heal the pain of family exile. Generosity between friends and family members is a great pill for the pain of family estrangement. So are gratitude and expressing your appreciation. As you continue coming to peace with yourself—learning from your family legacy as much what *not* to do as what to *do*—your capacity to feel and express these positive feelings will keep growing. The rewards will be incalculable.

10

Make Meaning out of
Your Experience

Ultimately, we achieve feelings of safety, inner security, and peace by what I call "making meaning" from our experience. However, when I talk about making meaning from the experience of family exile, I am not suggesting that you'll never again feel the pain of family estrangement. As with any trauma, the effects of a family rift change everyone involved forever— there will always be uncomfortable memories and emotional scars.

However, you can arrive at a place where the pain is manageable. You can recognize the times that make you feel terribly sad and upset (like Father's Day, Mother's Day, Christmas, or Thanksgiving) and prepare yourself for them. You will find you can tolerate these feelings, but at the same time remain functional and loving. You can handle the pain of family estrangement without resorting to self-defeating acting out. But most of all, you can use the experience to find and intensify meaning in your own life and thus experience a deeper measure of emotional security and sanity.

A client I'll call Ralph summed it up best as he approached the end of his therapy work with me. Ralph, a fifty-five-year-old architect in New York City, is happily married with two sons, age fourteen and sixteen. Ralph had married at thirty-seven and his parents were thrilled with his choice of Bonnie, a younger architect who had recently begun working in the same firm as he. They had been worried that their only son had waited so long to get married and were beginning to fear that he never would marry and have children.

"Well, the honeymoon between all of us ended within a year. Bonnie was pregnant with our first child. I was thrilled. My parents were thrilled until they asked Bonnie when she was going to stop working. Bonnie had no intention of giving up her career; my parents were outraged. They hurled all kinds of judgments and invective at both of us and my dad basically said that Bonnie was a bitch and I was a weak wimp. It was a terrible fight; I'll always remember it and cringe from the memory, and it's all been downhill since then.

"For the next fifteen years we struggled with them and had brief periods of estrangement that were briefly patched but the dysfunctional behavior prevailed and we continued to have the same fight over and over. I realized it was because my parents felt hurt by how differently we were living and bringing up our children—their grandchildren. My dad, who was now retired, felt increasingly diminished by both my and Bonnie's ongoing professional success, as well as, I believe, my good relationship with my two sons. Ultimately, the last fight we had was no different from any other, but this time I think all of us finally saw the futility of patching it up and setting ourselves up for more pain and, as we each saw it, abuse.

"That was three years ago. I realized early today that I've been acting and feeling really crazy and stressed for the last week and couldn't figure out why. I'm not sleeping well, I'm short-tempered and irritable, and I really thought I had no reason to feel this way. This morning I was doing my bank deposit and checked the date before filling out the deposit slip and wham—it hit me between the eyes: tomorrow is my mother's eightieth birthday. Well, I managed to continue what I was doing, but I felt like I was in a state of shock. I went back to my office, closed the door, and just started to cry. It's so tragic and sad. She's had a long life—it's been good in many ways and tragic in many others. She really didn't want this estrangement from us, and I'm sure she misses all of us a lot and that for a mother to be turning eighty and not have a relationship with her son and grandsons must be just awful; she must feel terribly like a failure. I know I would.

"My father really fueled the cutoff, and, as she's done for their whole married life, she went along passively with his insanity. She's just too weak to fight him or defy him, which makes me feel both enraged with her as well as tremendous compassion for her. Mostly, it just feels so, so sad and tragic for all of us. I can hardly tolerate thinking about it.

"After that I pulled myself together, called my wife, and told her what I realized about tomorrow's date, and that I was sorry I had been so crazy all week and that I loved her. I thought about how I was acting almost like my dad all week—cranky, full of resentment, and silently musing about how nobody really appreciated all I did. I realized that was crazy and I had a choice. I didn't have to behave or feel this way, and I thought about all the alternative modes of behavior I've learned in the last few years, and I set about putting them into practice.

"I went home that night, and, instead of isolating myself behind my computer or in front of the television, I played pool with my sons. In reality, they're both better pool players than me and overall better athletes. We played two games, and what was great about it was that each of them won one game. I reveled in that. My dad never let me win. He's never been happy when I've won. The fact that I could be so happy about my boys winning cast away any doubt I ever had about this entire struggle being worth it."

We can see from Ralph's story, along with so many others, that the pain of family estrangement and exile will never go away completely. At the same time we can see how Ralph's process was very much equivalent to going through the ten steps of healing that you've just gone through. He acknowledged the trauma; remembered the good life he had and could enjoy now; reflected on the roles his father, mother, and he had played throughout their lives; realized that without intending to he had taken on the resentful role of his father; reconnected to the gratitude he felt that he had a choice not to act destructively; and finally, with the help of a pool game with his sons, made meaning of the whole experience in a way that made it manageable. The happiness he now feels is deeper, more authentic. It doesn't eradicate his pain, but rather makes use of it to remind him, partly by contrast, of the very real blessings he enjoys in his life.

Our One Unassailable Freedom

Victor Frankl was a Viennese psychotherapist who founded a school of therapy called logotherapy, whose meaning derives from the Greek word *logos*, "to make meaning out of something." The central premise of logotherapy is that while we cannot control what happens to us in our lives, we can choose our attitude toward life's conditions and toward ourselves. The path to recovery, according to logotherapy, is literally to learn to make meaning out of whatever circumstances come our way in life—learn to reflect profitably on our experience so that we can frame it in a way that both mirrors reality and serves our most cherished aims.

Frankl, a young psychiatrist in Vienna before World War II, was, between 1942 and 1945, interred in a Nazi concentration camp. Partly because of this experience, he developed his theories of logotheraphy. He certainly confirms the lessons I've learned as a psychotherapist, as well as what I've learned as an individual struggling to come to terms with family estrangement. As he states, in his book *Man's Search for Meaning,* "This was the lesson I had to learn in three years spent at Auschwitz and Dachau: those most apt to survive the camps were those oriented toward the future, toward a meaning to be fulfilled by them in the future" (Frankl, 1985, p.37).

While we cannot, by any stretch, compare family estrangement to incarceration in a Nazi concentration camp, we can detect some similar themes: dealing with circumstances beyond our control that create perplexing and profound loss in our lives. Frankl explained that we can create meaning in our lives in three different ways: "by creating a work or doing a deed; by experiencing something or encountering someone; and by the attitude we take toward unavoidable suffering" (p.176). The one freedom that cannot "be taken from a man," Frankl writes, is "to choose one's attitude in any given set of circumstances, to choose one's own way" (p.104).

One of Frankl's central observations during his years at Dachau and Auschwitz was that the inmates most likely to survive were those who focused on the future, were committed to the quest of making meaning out of their circumstances, and were determined to move forward with gratitude and hope instead of bitterness and resentment. Ultimately, the same may be said of individuals that survive and conquer the dysfunction of family estrangement.

The Gift of Embracing Suffering

The imperative to embrace suffering when the only other choice is to disintegrate, collapse, fall apart, or die is a principle we find in many religions and spiritual teachings. Sacred texts and teachings abound in stories and liturgies devoted to illuminating the lasting transformation that can occur through the acceptance and embrace of the challenges we meet on life's path. For some of us, family estrangement may turn out to be the biggest challenge we'll have had to face in our lives. As bad as the pain of this challenge can be, spiritual teachers and psychologists alike tell us that embracing this pain can generate abundant gifts. When we deal with the pain, as you are now dealing with yours, and change our attitudes and behavior rather than attempting the impossible task of changing others, we can move on with grace, purpose, and serenity. The rewards of doing this go far beyond dealing with the family rift: we become blessed with an enhanced inner life, greater wisdom, and strength to help us face every new challenge in life.

Rabbi Yehudah Fine, author of *Times Square Rabbi*, wrote about the particular suffering and pain he faced after a near fatal automobile accident, referring to his time in recovery as "The Worst of Times and the Best of Times." He calls the ordeal of the car crash and his recovery a "Five Star Crisis." People who have had to come to terms with family estrangement, whether it results in reconciliation or not, might readily apply this phrase to their own experience.

While it's obvious why Fine refers in his title to this having been the worst of times, it may not be as clear why he says it's the best of times. He explains that "in the middle of the mystery of pain, there are precious jewels to be harvested. There are gifts of the heart to be experienced." And it is those gifts that I hope you will have received along the way, as has been true for me and many of my patients and the people I interviewed for this book. These gifts essentially recap the lessons we've learned through every step and chapter of this book. Let's look at some of these gifts now.

The Gift of Freedom, Autonomy, and Choice

We've seen above how Rabbi Fine made a choice to live and recover. Every person we've met in this book has made a choice to get through their estrangement one way or another, either to mend the family rift or to learn to feel good about themselves despite their family's inability to reunite. This is what Victor Frankl was referring to when he talked about the freedom to choose your own attitude in the face of suffering. The family that cuts off is a family that doesn't allow for choice, and therefore tends to generate what is, at times, a crippling lack of autonomy—thwarting by ridicule and punitiveness any individual family member's attempt to make decisions.

The benefit of greater personal freedom, independence, and choice is illustrated by a client of mine. Anna cannot remember a time when she wasn't at angry cross-purposes with her sister Martina. After years of putting up with what Anna felt was intolerable abuse—"I couldn't express an opinion about anything without Martina jumping down my throat"—she finally felt she'd had enough. "The feeling of 'that's it' was so complete, and amazingly I felt no rancor. I just didn't want to continue a relationship with my sister that always ended in her hurling invective at me for no reason."

When Martina called Anna and began to deliver her weekly tirade, Anna simply replied, "I'm sorry you feel that way. Please call me when you feel differently." Anna says she wasn't angry; she simply felt very certain that she was right to protect herself in this way against her sister's unending barbs. "I could hear Martina gasp in fury," Anna says, "and I gently said goodbye and hung up the phone." It wasn't that Anna felt no anxiety about taking the risk she had taken—but she continued to feel she was right to have taken it.

Every time Martina attempted to call Anna and lay into her, Anna repeated the same unwillingness to talk. Finally Martina sent her a scathing letter that said she'd never contact her sister again. There followed a year of silence between the two sisters.

"I wasn't thrilled about this," Anna says, "but I did a lot of work on myself in that year and realized that I had kowtowed not only to my sister my whole life, but pretty much to everyone else, too. I realize I had backed down ever since I was a little girl—I really had become my family's doormat. So I'd done something really major by refusing to take abuse from Martina—something that had good repercussions in the rest of my life. But after a while, I realized I did still care about and missed Martina. I mean, she's the only sister I have. So finally I summoned up the courage to call her, a good year and a half after we'd ceased all contact. I still did want a relationship with her.

"She answered the phone, and I said, 'Hi, Martina. I miss you. I just wanted to see how you and your family are doing.' Martina first was speechless," Anna said, "but then she very calmly told me she was glad I'd called, that she missed me, that she'd had some time to think about how pushy she guessed she sometimes was, and in fact was thinking of calling me."

The point of this story isn't to suggest that happy outcomes are guaranteed when one family member takes the risk of contacting another after a period of silence, but to underscore the real success for Anna—which was to discover that she could make a solo decision that served her best interests and stick to it. She had gained a crucial inner strength by acting autonomously—for herself, without fearing what anyone else would think about it. Maybe it was this strength, conveyed by the calm in her voice when she called her sister, that engendered the beginning of a change in Martina, too. Sometimes your own sense of well-being radiates out to others—and they begin to want some, too.

The Gift of Tolerance

Thinking about how people can make meaning out of family relationships, I reflect on my work and how clients of mine have been able to find meaning in their own family experiences through psychotherapy. However, there's something much more powerful than any professional ability I may have to give back what I've learned. That's the satisfaction I personally derive from my own family relationships—the family of my wife and children and my extended second-chance family of relatives and friends. That's where the most genuine meaning resides—a meaning that is available to all of us. To derive this meaning, it is crucial to develop tolerance for human fallibility and difference.

Ezra, another of my clients, said it beautifully: "I've become a much more tolerant and understanding person. I like that in myself. I wasn't raised to be sympathetic to the struggles of other people or to be open-minded about possibilities when there's a conflict between family members or friends.

"But now I find I like being sensitive and compassionate to the people in my world. That covers a broad gamut of situations, ranging from being tolerant of people who are different from me in terms of race, class, or ethnicity, as well as understanding everyone's human mistakes and confusion. I give the benefit of the doubt to others nowadays, and like myself so much more than when I was quick to judge people and to overreact to what in my judgment I perceived to be malevolent."

Ezra realizes this tolerance came late to him. "When my son married outside our religion, I reacted in a completely self-referential, and frankly, unpleasant way. Ultimately, my son and I didn't speak to each other for a year after the marriage until my daughter-in-law became pregnant and my hard-hearted stance finally abated. I learned a lot during that time, and I'm grateful that my son and his wife took a nonjudgmental and generous stand toward my wanting to rekindle the relationship.

"But you don't just develop tolerance once and have done with it. New situations arise to test you. For example, recently I was supposed to meet my cousin and his wife for dinner, but they had gotten into an enormous fight and my cousin didn't show up. I ended up hearing about their bad marriage from his wife, and I was angry and expected an apology from my cousin. I thought for sure he would feel mortified and awful about being such a jerk, and that would prompt him to call me the next day. Well, he didn't, and my head of steam worked up more. By the day after, I thought to myself my cousin's gone off the deep end and isn't speaking to me. I was very hurt and upset.

"Three days later, he called. In the old days, I would have put him through hoops to convince me he was contrite. He would have apologized, and I would have made it clear that a simple apology was not enough—an intolerance I always saw in my mother, who was incapable of bearing any hint of a slight or rebuff without extracting endless 'I'm sorry's.' No wonder she had so few friends. But this time, something softened in me. I found myself saying, 'Don't worry. It's over.' I made a joke about how if it happened again, I'd come over and 'kick his ass.' And then I said, 'Let's put it away. Everyone has a bad day. How are you now?' "

The Gift of Empowerment

Another client, Andrea, talked about the empowerment she felt having survived estrangement from her grown and only son due to his involvement in a therapy cult that advocated cutting all ties with the family. "It's sad," Andrea said, "like a premature accidental death of a young person would be. Clive's had emotional problems since his early twenties and had gone from therapist to therapist, never seeming to be able to get better. When he found this therapist who is part of this weird cult with a philosophy that family estrangement is curative, he cut us off completely.

"My husband got solace in the Church, and I went to therapy, but together we came to an understanding that human life is very precious and family connection probably means more than any other connection. That's allowed me to be a much better parent to my other children and go to great lengths to build a sense of connection with them. I still feel heartsick about Clive, but somehow the powerlessness I feel to change him has increased the sense of empowerment I feel in the people in my family to whom I can show love."

Facing your powerlessness to change others can in fact be empowering—teaching you whom you do have the ability to help and reach through your love, and whom you do not. This is one of many paradoxical lessons of healing from a family rift. By empowered, I mean the ability to contend in a serene manner with life's inevitable interpersonal crises, family calamities, relationship dramas, and parent-child predicaments. With this kind of empowerment, you are able to navigate these terrains in a way that builds up relationships and makes them stronger. That's *real* power—as opposed to the illusory power of cutting a family member out of your life.

The Gift of Gratitude

I've talked a great deal about gratitude and generosity in this book because cultivating a sense of gratitude is so central to living a meaningful and complete life, unfettered by neurotic symptoms and free of the burdens of our past. This has been evident in all of the success stories we've explored in this book: each person who has managed to heal from the wounds of a family rift has also managed to experience an increased and heightened sense of being grateful for his or her blessings. There is no room for bitterness in gratitude: it eradicates the negative and opens the heart to the positive.

Gratitude is also often what allows for mending a family estrangement. Some years ago, a client, Vivian, came to see me because she felt uncomfortable about her relationship with her aging father. She hadn't had any contact with him since she was nineteen, some thirty years before, because she had had an abortion, of which her parents had violently disapproved.

"My uncle was a priest, my grandparents were devout Catholics, and so were my mother and father. They just completely wrote me off. It was horrible, and it's taken years for me to get over the pain of having been so completely dismissed, especially by my grandparents whom I loved so much when I was a child—who gave me the only real affection and attention I'd received as a child." Vivian adjusted, married, had a family—and managed to find joy and purpose in her life.

But then, out of the blue, she got a call from her father that shook her world. "He told me my mother had just died. I lost it—just broke down completely on the phone. I could hear how much he missed me. He joined me in crying, telling me he hoped I'd come back now and see him." Vivian was deeply rocked by the experience, not least because as much as she'd longed for her family rift to heal, she also had spent so many years furious at her father. "I both craved seeing him and never wanted to see him again."

Then Vivian had a dream she related to me. "I was sitting down to dinner with my husband and kids, but the strange thing was that we were all the same age, all in our early twenties. Suddenly the door opened and a man came in carrying a platter shaped as fish with loaves of bread on it. I thought it was weird, and the man disappeared after he put down the platter. No one commented, and I started eating. Then I woke up feeling ravenous. I don't understand it." When we spoke about the dream, Vivian realized the fish platter and loaves of bread referred to the biblical story and that the old man must have been a reference to her father.

I pointed out to Vivian that in the dream, her father was generous and nurturing. "Yes, he was, at least in the ways that he could be. He loved to cook, and it was always a real treat when he cooked for the family." I asked Vivian if she might have more positive and loving memories of her dad than she liked to admit.

With that, she began tearing up and talked about the many things about her father she loved as a child, and how in many ways, he was nurturing and generous. "I think that's what's bugging me. As much as he and my mother turned their backs on me after the abortion, before that he was always as generous as circumstances allowed him to be. I'm grateful for that, and I guess I feel underneath my stubbornness that I need to acknowledge that—and be generous back to him. Mostly I realize I still love him very much."

It doesn't take much gratitude to open the floodgates to love—and allow bygones to be bygones. Vivian says that it was as much her gratitude to her own family now that motivated her to allow her father back into her heart as it was gratitude to her dad. "They've taught me the power of being thankful, because they've given me so much to be thankful for. Somehow, now, that transfers over to my dad and me."

The Gift of Generosity

Elizabeth, a woman whom I was privileged to interview for this book, told me the following touching and instructive story. "When my daughter and son-in-law divorced, I tried very hard to maintain a good relationship with her ex-husband. After all, he was my grandchildren's father. Unfortunately, this was difficult given the enmity between the two of them. However, my daughter had custody of the children, so they were around a great deal of the time in their early years, and my husband and I were deeply involved in their lives.

"When my daughter was killed by a drunken driver three years ago, it was shattering for us and for the children. They were six and eight and really counted on us and their mother, given the limited relationship they had with their father. He had by that point remarried and was living with his new wife and her children. My husband and I offered to let the kids move in with us, but my son-in-law wanted them to come live with him and his new family, and we had to accede to his wishes.

"The tragic premature death of my daughter was followed by two other terrible events, all of which seemed unimaginable to me. My husband died of a heart attack three months after her death, and that was followed by my son-in-law announcing that he was moving clear across the country with his new family, which of course included my grandchildren. I was shattered by these events and wondered if I could survive them. In the space of a year, I went from having an active family life with my husband, daughter, and grandchildren to being completely alone and without family in my day-to-day life.

"Things then went from bad to worse. My daughter's marriage had ended because her husband was a gambler. She couldn't and wouldn't tolerate his addiction and chronic debt. When my son-in-law found out that the inheritance she had left for their children from a modest life insurance policy had been put in trust for them with me as the guardian, he was outraged. He felt I should sign the money over to him since he was now responsible for their upbringing and education.

"I refused because I feared he'd gamble their money away, and I wanted it conserved for their college education. Well, this created an irreparable breach between us, and he began refusing to let the children speak to me on the phone. When I invited them to visit me, and even sent plane tickets, my invitation and the tickets were returned to me, unopened.

"I had always been a positive, optimistic, and upbeat person, and I felt I had overcome many difficulties in my life, but being kept from any relationship with my grandchildren, on top of the loss of my daughter and husband, felt like it would kill me. I began to get depressed and found it difficult to get myself motivated to do anything. Then I read an article about Mother's Against Drunk Driving, a group of parents who had lost children to drunken driving accidents and were lobbying for stricter laws about driving while under the influence of alcohol.

"I went to a meeting and met other people who had lost their children in this tragic way, and I volunteered to work in their offices. Well, this has saved my life. I began thinking, if I can prevent one child's death from drunken driving, I will have a reason to go on after all the tragedies of recent years. Ultimately, I've devoted myself to MADD, and I've also developed a great network of support and friendship with other parents who have weathered similar tragedies.

"I haven't given up hope about connecting with my grandchildren, although their father has continued to boycott me and still tries to blackmail me to release the children's money to him, which I feel would be wrong to do to them and disrespectful to my daughter's wishes. Plus, if he can be this heartless and unloving to his children as to deprive them of connection with me—their mother's only living family—I assume he'd still keep them apart from me even if I succumbed to his blackmail.

"So when I'm steamrollered by all of this and my feelings of being bereft over the loss of my entire family threaten to overtake me, I focus on helping others and contributing something back to the world. After all, I lost a great deal in recent years, but I haven't lost my memories, and I am grateful for all the years I was surrounded by a wonderful and loving family."

Elizabeth's discovery of generosity—the generosity of giving her time to a cause that has great meaning to her—has saved her from this terrible family rift in ways that she could never have anticipated. This is one of the most sterling examples I have encountered of finding meaning in one's life. And it underscores, once again, just how personally healing the experience of giving to others can be. It has done nothing less than allow Elizabeth to tolerate what might otherwise be the unbearable pain of family cutoffs caused by death and her son-in-law's intransigence.

The Gift of Acceptance

"Life is so much easier when you can accept people for who they are. I had to really struggle to learn this, and it took me well over a decade to do so, but now at least I don't have to keep trying to do the impossible: change the people I love." These are the words of Frida, a friend of mine who talks about her struggle to accept the people around her for who they are as well as learning to accept herself.

"I grew up feeling miserable, lonely, and depressed with an alcoholic mother and a depressed father. It wasn't until I went to Al-Anon that I learned how to deal with them. They didn't like it when I began to get better—well, mostly my mother didn't like it. Sadly, she couldn't tolerate my growth and increasing unwillingness to tolerate her abusiveness. We were estranged when she died. So now I struggle every day to accept my husband and my children for who they are. When I succeed, I feel much better for two reasons: One is that I feel more successful because I'm not failing at a task that is inherently impossible. The other reason I feel better is my relationships are better and I get more pleasure and gratification from the people I love most in the world."

However, it has definitely been a struggle getting to the stance of acceptance she now embraces and finds so healing. "You'd think after having been so unaccepted by my family, especially my mother, growing up, that I'd be the most tolerant person in the world now. But boy, I sure haven't been." Frida received what she said was a double-whammy from her son and daughter—the former, who announced he was gay; the latter, who had decided to marry a man from Pakistan and was considering converting to Islam.

"Suddenly I turned into my mother. I blew up at them. I actually heard myself say the words, 'How could you do this to me?' as if these personal life decisions they needed and wanted to make were somehow really aimed at bothering me. But what shocked me most was how quickly I reverted to the judgmentalism I'd seen in my mother. Now I found myself accused of homo-phobia and racism—and was threatened by both my children with the pros-pect of never seeing them again if I didn't apologize."

Frida was humbled by this, and had to do some heavy soul-searching to realize what had happened. "I'd blown up purely by reflex—a reflex I didn't know I even had. It seemed to come whole out of my mother. For those moments, the moments my children made their announcements to me, I think I felt exactly as my mother would have felt—that everything that didn't go her way was somehow meant to kick her in the teeth. She took every disap-pointment so personally. And here I was doing the same thing.

"It's turned out to be hard work achieving acceptance of my kids' deci-sions—even after I made the connection that I was being the worst parts of my mother. I suppose my son and daughter made me see I really had had a kind of vision of who I thought they were 'supposed' to be. But now, over time, the painful memory of my own estrangement from my mother has made me determined to do *anything and everything* humanly possible to accept my children for who they are. That's what I so longed for from my mother. And that's the kind of acceptance I'm now determined, with a full and giving heart, to extend to my kids."

The Gift of Wisdom

All the qualities we've explored in this chapter and throughout this book—all the gifts and benefits—might be summarized and encapsulated by the word *wisdom*. However, we each need to come to our understanding of wisdom in individual ways. We find the wisdom we need to find, and it will inevitably derive from and apply to such factors as our different places in the life cycle, gender, family histories, relationships, cultures, assumptions, dreams, hopes, and fears.

Every reader of this book can attest that information is not the same as wisdom. You can have encyclopedic knowledge of facts and not one whit of understanding, common sense, compassion—or wisdom. And the wisdom you derive from your family estrangement isn't something you could have acquired just anywhere or from anyone else. No book or pundit knows as much as you do about the particular family rift challenges you've had to face and what they've taught and are teaching you.

By wisdom, I refer to the capacity to use acquired information and knowledge to arrive at sound, intelligent, and prudent decisions. Frida referred to it when she talked about how the estrangement from her mother provided her with the wisdom to ensure that she didn't become estranged from her own children. All of us who have survived a family cutoff—and allowed ouselves to reflect on its impacts—can attest to having achieved greater wisdom about the process not only of dealing with the family rift but with many other challenges of life. When you've dealt with the trauma of a family rift, you can deal with almost anything.

The Gift of Humility

Yet another of the major gifts I've received from my struggles to recover from my family rift has been humility. The cliché "the more you know, the less you realize you know" has a great deal of truth. Indeed, the wiser you become, the more you realize you don't "know it all." Once again, the quality of humility is lacking in individuals who cut anyone out of their lives. Cutters often assume they do know it all—which is tantamount to saying that they have shut down in terms of receptivity. If only cutters, estrangers, could acquire humility and the wisdom to stop knowing it all, perhaps all family estrangements could be healed. Humility means receptivity, openness—a willingness to keep learning about yourself and others, a refusal to leap to judgment.

Humility is particularly crucial in my profession. People often expect that therapists are endowed with an infallible, all-knowing expertise. We are frequently idealized by our clients and sometimes vulnerable to believing and incorporating their high opinion of us into a grandiose self-view in our professional and personal lives. However, if we fall into believing in our own absolute authority or consider others' idealization of us to be valid and factual, we're no longer in the position of being able to heal others, for we're stuck in what amounts to our own spiritual sickness.

In a tragic example, Melanie Klein, one of the leading psychoanalytic theoreticians of the twentieth century, died without having reconciled and mended a relationship with her long-estranged only daughter, Melitta Schmideberg. She dismissed and minimized Melitta's feelings about her by interpreting them as having to do only with her inborn drives, dismissing any notion that Melitta had some valid feelings of disappointment and upset with her mother. She couldn't give up her role as authority and expert, and this lack of humility deprived her of one of the potentially most gratifying relationships of her life.

The Gift of Vision

We almost always undergo a kind of psychological blindness about ourselves when we've gone through a family estrangement. However, as we work through the steps of healing, we slowly have our sight restored to us. After having done everything in your power to change a family relationship for the better without success, you will eventually see that your relatives' problems and issues are not about you.

Naomi, a sixty-year-old mother of three grown daughters, recently told me about her struggles with her oldest child. "Ruth and I were estranged for six months, and I felt just awful about her not speaking with me. We've finally reached a truce and have been seeing each other and speaking with each other, but it's difficult for both of us. On my birthday, we almost had another blowout, but I managed to back off and let go of my resentment about the fact that she and her husband planned a family trip that weekend.

"I like my birthday and it's important to me, but this was a real milestone, and not such an easy day for me either. Sixty is a significant age, after all, and I couldn't believe Ruth was not going to be around to celebrate with the rest of us. Anyway, I was able to focus on how great a time I'd have with my other daughters and their families, and how lucky I was overall to have such great kids and six grandchildren to boot.

"My other daughters kept reminding me, too, that Ruth had always been like this and is like this with everyone, and that it's not about me. Of course, her neglect of me tends to be more dramatic a lot of the time, because I'm her mother, but she can easily blow up and dismiss anyone for what she perceives to be any critical or wounding statement directed at her. And with me, as well as her sisters, she dwells on a lifetime of hurts and angers that keep coming back up for her.

"I guess I've finally realized that it's really out of my control if she can't let go of them. I've apologized for everything she feels I did wrong as a mother, and acknowledged to her the ways in which I believe she's got legitimate gripes. And yet she can't let go of them. I hope she will. But I've done what I can, what's humanly possible to repair our relationship, and any enmity at this point, any perceived wound against her, is truly not about me. It's about her.

"That understanding really helped me. When I was with her last week, I saw something amazing about her and how she operates. She and her family were about to leave after a visit. My grandchildren gave me a big hug and kiss goodbye, as did my son-in-law, and then Ruth came and stood right in front of me to say goodbye—no hug, not even a handshake. She's not affectionate or warm. It's who she is, and, once again, I realized it's not about me. Well, seeing and understanding that, I found myself able to put my arms around her and kiss her cheek and say goodbye and tell her, 'I love you.' It was great for me to feel comfortable doing that, and I think it may have been pretty good for her too.

"What I realize is that I've been given a twofold gift of vision. Not only can I see myself more clearly in this relationship for the first time, but also I can for the first time really see Ruth for who she is. It amounts to losing some psychological blindness I guess I've always had until that moment. I'm grateful for that."

The Gift of Self-Esteem

My sense about the ways in which I've learned to make meaning out of the experience of family estrangement could be summed up as a feeling that I have decided to become the best "me" I can be. Until I had dealt with my family, I really don't think I had achieved anywhere near my full capacity as a human being, or the higher level of self-esteem that comes with that. Sadly, for my father and many injustice collectors, their maneuvering and decision to exile a family member depends upon attacking that family member's self-esteem. "If you weren't such a . . . [fill in the blank], I wouldn't be doing this."

The only way to understand family exile from the point of view of the injustice collector is to see that the exiled family member is held to be completely and totally in the wrong. There's no other possible interpretation to the injustice collector. This kind of wholesale negative judgment is not designed to make the exiles feel very good about themselves.

Every person I've ever talked to who has dealt with issues of resentment and forgiveness reports that forgiveness always wins out: there are only benefits to giving up grievances and moving on in life. When I think back on the years I spent intermittently being consumed with rage toward my family and their treatment of me, I think of how much more productive I could have been and how I might have felt a much greater sense of well-being earlier in life if I had learned these lessons. I can forgive myself because I know I needed to go through the process of struggle and learning I've gone through to get where I am today. We all do.

I hope if you've learned nothing else from this book, that you've arrived at a place of forgiveness toward yourself, and that you are benefiting from the increased feelings of well-being and self-esteem this forgiveness always bestows. Those of us who grew up in families that were not forgiving—families, unlike our second-chance families, who did not permit second chances—need to make self-forgiveness and the bolstering of self-esteem an ongoing priority and practice. This takes vigilance. It is too easy to revert to harsh self-criticism when something goes wrong, and by ancient reflex become sure once again that "it's all my fault." It's too easy to fall back to judging ourselves just as ruthlessly as we were evaluated by our injustice-collecting families. Great care must be taken not to revert to this old, terribly self-destructive rut.

One way of treating yourself with this necessary care is to remember the "self-esteem workshop" list we learned about in Chapter 2: the list of your positive qualities that I encouraged you to itemize (e.g., friendly, generous, persevering, appreciative of others, competent, resourceful, creative, humorous, loving, thoughtful, strong, able to handle crises, compassionate). As with the gratitude list we returned to in the last chapter, you'll likely find that as you make this list now you can add more traits than you could when you first itemized it. Give it a try—and keep the list you write in your pocket, wallet, or purse. Consult it often. Add to it when you feel the urge—which, as you continue healing, you will.

The Gift of Love

Telling a child, parent, or sibling that you never will speak to them again as long as you live, that they're no longer welcome in your home, that you're writing them off as dead because of your perceptions of their behaviors or the choices they've made in life is, I believe, one of the most unloving acts imaginable. Yet fortunately for us, as we undergo the process of healing from our family rifts, we experience an increased capacity to be loving, to feel loving, to act in a loving way toward others. This is perhaps the biggest benefit any of my clients have talked about receiving as they recover from family rift wounds. It's certainly the biggest benefit I've been fortunate enough to receive.

This is a response and outcome I've heard from many of the people whom I interviewed for this book as well. The work you've done has allowed you to be a more loving and kind person, probably more loving, generous, and genuine than you've ever allowed yourself to be in your life.

That is how it has worked for me. I treat my wife, children, and friends better than I did before confronting and dealing with the estrangement from my family. I'm more tolerant, understanding, and generous with my affection and feelings of positive regard. For me this has generated huge returns of love, and for this I feel grateful. Realize that you can count on receiving the same gift.

Index